The concept of dwelling

JANKE

Christian
Norberg-Schulz

The concept
of dwelling

On the way
to figurative architecture

Electa/RIZZOLI
NEW YORK

Cover
"Between earth and sky."
Drawing by J. Utzon

Library of Congress Cataloging in Publication Data
Norberg-Schulz, Christian.
    The concept of dwelling.
    Includes bibliographies.
    1. Architecture-Environmental aspects. 2. Architecture-
Human factors. 3. Architecture-Philosophy.
I. Title.
NA2542.35.N6713   1985   720   84-43110
ISBN 0-8478-0590-5

First published in 1985 in the United States of America by
RIZZOLI INTERNATIONAL PUBLICATIONS, INC.
597 Fifth Avenue, New York, New York 10017

This volume was originally published in Italian
© 1984 Electa Editrice, Milan
Printed in Italy

Contents

To Anna Maria

Foreword

This is a book on human dwelling. The word "dwelling" here means something more than having a roof over our head and a certain number of square meters at our disposal. First, it means to meet others for exchange of products, ideas and feelings, that is, to experience life as a multitude of possibilities. Second, it means to come to an agreement with others, that is, to accept a set of common values. Finally, it means to be oneself, in the sense of having a small chosen world of our own. We may call these modes collective, public and private dwelling.

The word dwelling, however, also comprises the places man has created to set the modes into his work. The settlement, with its urban spaces, has always been the stage where collective dwelling was enacted. The institution or public building has been the embodiment of public dwelling. And the house has been the private retreat where the individual could prosper. Together, settlement, urban space, institution and house constitute a total environment. This environment, however, is always related to what is given, that is, to a landscape with general as well as particular qualities. To dwell, therefore, also means to become friends with a natural place.

We may also say that dwelling consists in orientation and identification. We have to know where we are and how we are, to experience existence as meaningful. Orientation and identification are satisfied by organized space and built form, which together constitute the concrete place. Our introduction of the concept of place, in contrast to the current emphasis on abstract space, offers a point of departure for a return to *figurative* architecture.

Thus we leave the "non-figurative" approach of functionalism behind, and open up for an architecture which may satisfy the need for dwelling, in the existential sense of the word. When dwelling is accomplished, our wish for belonging and participation is fulfilled.

Christian Norberg-Schulz

7

In the short story *Last man home* the Norwegian writer Tarjei Vesaas tells about Knut, a youngster who is out in the forest to fell timber.[1] He has participated many times before, but today he suddenly understands what it means. *"Here you are at home, Knut."* What? Nobody had spoken. But it is this that is happening today: "Here you are at home." A wonderful, true and simple world is opened up just here, where he is born. Like a precious gift. He moves about among the trees that have been felled, and the thousand which are still standing. Something happens to him today: The forest discloses itself. His own place is revealed. This is an important day for a human being. Therefore Knut becomes "last man home." The others leave, but he has to remain to see "how the great forest prepares itself for the night. To see how the darkness leaks out of the ground, from the sky, from the horizon. He is spellbound. He does not know what happens to him, but feels that he has to remain in the forest his whole life — if his life should be right and true." Knut, therefore, does not remain just to experience the forest, but to find *himself*.

"This evening is like an initiation, like being dedicated to a life among trees and taciturn people... And still there is nothing which makes this evening different from the evening yesterday or the day before... Yesterday it was the same. And the day before. And last year. And when *father* was young, the forest was the same. But tonight it is something new, for Knut. Tonight he senses everything as it is: a great kinship. He has grown out of these hills and valleys and the flowing water. Here he is a fruit himself. A child.

Tonight the mind is open like a bowl." Vesaas' story tells about what it means to "be at home," Knut suddenly experiences what it is to know a place, to belong to a place. And he realizes that this place has conditioned his own being, his personality. The locality discloses itself to him, and thereby "his own place." Life becomes "right and true" because of this relationship; it becomes *meaningful*. Vesaas furthermore suggests that the disclosure consists in the experience of concrete qualities. Knut *knows* the forest, he knows how it is to move about among the trees, he knows the humming of the wind, he has seen how the dusk leaks forth. He remains to get the confirmation of what he spontaneously perceived when the forest whispered: "here you are at home." Thus he is "caught" by the forest, and even if he should settle somewhere else later in life, the forest will always be with him. It is important to point out that Vesaas does not describe a *particular* place. He presents the forest as a *typical* environment we find in many localities, and which concerns many human beings. We do infer that he has the Norwegian coniferous forest in mind, but a foreign reader who knows another kind of wood, will easily grasp the meaning. Indeed, he could have written a similar tale about any kind of environment; about the desert or the steppe, about the coast or the mountains. The theme is general, and Vesaas only presents in poetical form what we imply when we say: "I am a forester," or "I am a highlander." When we thus identify ourselves, we use the place as our reference. The particular place is part of the identity of each individual, and since the place belongs to a type, one's identity is also general. Vesaas furthermore suggests what is

basic in the experience of a place. Thus he uses the words "ground," "sky," and "horizon" to indicate its content. *All* places are determined by the ground on which we stand, by the sky above our heads, and by the limit of the horizon. But the character of the ground varies. Knut has heather and moss under his feet, while other men walk on sand or stone. The sky is also different; in the South it appears as a high dome with a burning sun, whereas in the North it is often a "low" and misty veil through which light is filtered. And the appearance of the horizon is determined by the local topography and vegetation. These changing conditions are experienced in relation to day, night and seasons. Vesaas, however, emphasizes that the result is not a series of transient impressions. He describes the place as something *permanent*, which was the same yesterday and last year, and even when father was young. In mentioning the father, Vesaas also implies that Knut's experience is nothing merely personal. It is an objective "truth" which is accessible to everybody, if only the mind is open. When that is the case, existence becomes what it "is." Therefore Vesaas says that Knut receives a "precious gift." This gift is something he *shares* with others. The writer explicitly talks about a "life between trees and taciturn people." The place, therefore, unites a group of human beings, it is something which gives them a common identity and hence a basis for a fellowship or society. The *permanence* of the place is what enables it to play this role. In the title of the story Vesaas also refers to another "home," and at the end of the tale Knut "goes home." He is certainly "at home" in the forest, but still he needs a *house*, a dwelling, in the usual sense of the word. In another

1. Norwegian forest.

text Vesaas tells us what the house means to us: "The faithful heart does not like to ramble about without a homestead. It needs a fixed spot to return to, it wants its square house."[2] "Human beings live there, and invisible rings are created by human radiation; they enclose and invite, delimit and open gates. The one who has built for himself such a fixed point may also approach it from the outside, and return to it as if to a new gift." Again Vesaas uses the word "gift"; the house is also a gift, like the experienced world around. This gift consists in the "radiation" created by the builder of the house. The writer explains it with these words: "Here the human heart has blossomed and the mind has mused." ...and therefore, "my house stands here and sings..." The result of the blossoming of heart and brain, thus, is a house that "sings," a house which radiates something to the surroundings, and into which we enter to receive the gift of its song.

The house is not a "given" place like the forest; it is man-made, and its message therefore seems to be of a different kind. But Vesaas suggests that there exists an interdependence between the house and environment. Thus he says that the house "stands solidly on the ground," "as if asleep under the winds of the sky." The house, accordingly, has something to do with earth and sky: "On the wide, waste slope, where nature unfolds in harmony, the lonely house stands, taking up a kind of strife with the surroundings; it may win and triumph, but may also helplessly lose." Vesaas evidently does not mean that the "victory" of the house consists in dominating nature, but rather in its "standing solidly on the ground," so that "friendly dusk may gather around it." When Knut returns to the house, he therefore does not come to a place which is different from the meaningful world outside, but to an inner world in harmony with the outer one. "The green ground is where I have my home, my fixed point." "And it does not have to be green either, it is found in the urban street as well." Although Vesaas first of all was familiar with natural places and rural houses, he realized that the same relationship is found in the city.

Finally, he suggests that the house has a social meaning: "Both woman and man would like to have a place to be united, as everywhere on Earth." Furthermore houses belong together, like members of a family. "Your house and my house look friendly to each other when it is right. When it is right, there is sympathy between houses."

In a forceful way Vesaas tells us what it means to *dwell*, in the true sense of the word. Today we usually define dwelling as having a roof over one's head and a certain number of square meters at disposal. That is, we understand the concept of dwelling in material and quantitative terms. Vesaas, however, gives the concept a *qualitative*, existential interpretation. To dwell means to belong to a given place, which might be a green field or a grey street, and furthermore to possess a house where the heart may blossom and the mind muse. These two homes belong together; when we enter our house we bring the outer world along — it is after all part of our identity and conditions our being. In the house this interdependence is expressed: "The house stands there, singing..." The house sings about how the inhabitant has a managed to come to terms with his environment; it radiates what he has obtained from being in the world. Some houses are mute, some shout. Others sing, and we behold their song.

To dwell in the qualitative sense is a basic condition of humanity. When we identify with a place, we dedicate ourselves to a way of being in the world. Therefore dwelling demands something from us, as well as from our places. *We* have to have an open mind, and the *places* have to offer rich possibilities for identification.

I. Dwelling and existence

Being-in-the-world

To dwell implies the establishment of a meaningful relationship between man and a given environment. In the introduction we have suggested that this relationship consists in an act of identification, that is, in a sense of belonging to a certain place. Man, thus, finds himself when he *settles*, and his being-in-the-world is thereby determined. On the other hand, man is also a wanderer. As *homo viator*, he is always on the way, which implies a possibility of choice. He chooses his place, and hence a certain kind of fellowship with other men. This dialectic of departure and return, of path and goal, is the essence of that existential "spatiality" which is set into work by architecture.[3]

It is the profound poetical theme of Saint-Exupéry's *Citadelle*, where we read: "I am a builder of cities, I have stopped the caravan on its way. It was only a seed-corn in the wind. But I resist the wind and bury the seed in the earth, to make cedars grow to the honor of God."[4]

In Saint-Exupéry's book man's environment is presented as a desert, to emphasize that settling means to cultivate and take care of the earth. We could also say that human existence is qualified by the insoluble unity of life and place.

The four modes of dwelling

The *settlement* is the first place of dwelling which has to be discussed in our investigation. Evidently this implies a study of the given natural environment, since a settlement, can only be understood in relation to its surroundings. The settlement, therefore, is the stage where *natural dwelling* takes place.

It might be objected that it hardly happens today that human beings have the opportunity to settle in a virgin land, and that the problem therefore is of mere historical interest. In our time we are from birth "thrown" into a pre-existing, man-made environment, to which we have to adapt, often without much possibility of choice. This is certainly true, but an already existing place also has to be understood as a settlement, that is, as an answer to the original problem of finding a foothold in a given world. And the construction of a new building within an old context is also, in a certain sense, an act of settling.

When settling is accomplished, other modes of dwelling which concern basic forms of human togetherness, come into play. The settlement functions as a place of encounter, where men may exchange products, ideas and sentiments. From ancient times *urban space* has been the stage where human meeting takes place. Meeting does not necessarily imply agreement; primarily it means that human beings come together in their diversities. Urban space, thus, is essentially a place of discovery, a "milieu of possibilities." In urban space man "dwells" in the sense of experiencing the richness of a world. We may call this mode *collective dwelling*, using the word "collective" in the original sense of gathering or assembly.

When choices are made within the milieu of possibilities, patterns of agreement are established, which represent a more structured kind of togetherness than the mere meeting. Agreement thus implies common interests or values, and forms the basis for a fellowship or society. An agreement also has to "take place," in the sense of possessing a forum where the common values are kept and expressed. Such a place is generally known as an *institution* or public building, and the mode of dwelling it serves we may call *public dwelling*, using the word "public" to denote what is shared by the community. Since the public building embodies a set of beliefs or values, it ought to appear as an "explanation," which makes the common world visible.

Choices, however, are also of a more personal kind, and the life of each individual has its particular course. Dwelling therefore also comprises that withdrawal which is necessary to define and develop one's own identity. We may call this mode *private dwelling*, intending those actions which are secluded from the intrusion of others. It ought to be pointed out that seclusion here implies withdrawal rather than unusual actions, since private life also follows established, common patterns.

The stage where private dwelling takes place, is the *house* or home, which may be characterized as a "refuge" where man gathers and expresses those memories which make up his personal world.

Settlement, urban space, institution and house constitute the total environment, where natural, collective, public and private dwelling take place. Our investigation has to consider all these levels, taking the existential structures which determine the four modes of dwelling as the point of departure. The study thereby gets a human basis, although not in conventional psychological or sociological terms. The problem of dwelling, however, is not exhausted when the four modes and their related architectural levels have been studied. To arrive at a *general* understanding of dwelling, we also have to ask whether the modes have a common denominator. To answer this question, we have to return to our point of departure: the concept of identification.

3. The four modes of dwelling: Bamberg 1493.

The two aspects of dwelling

In general, identification means to experience a "total" environment as meaningful. Within such a totality, however, certain things necessarily stand forth as particularly significant, or, in Gestalt terms, as "figures" on a less structured "ground."[5] In the Vesaas passages "forest" and "house" possess this quality. The objects of man's identification obviously are these things. At the same time he orientates among them, to be able to carry out his actions.[6] We could also say that man's being-in-the-world comprises a *how* as well as a *where*. While identification intends the qualities of things, orientation grasps their spatial interrelationship. Obviously we may orientate among things without really identifying with them, and we may also identify with certain qualities without fully involving the function of orientation. It is therefore meaningful to distinguish between identification and orientation as aspects of dwelling, and although both are always present, one of them may, according to the situation, be stronger than the other. Together identification and orientation make up the general structure of dwelling and hence the common denominator of the four modes.

It follows from what has been said before, that identification is related to bodily form, whereas orientation apprehends spatial order. We could also say that they correspond to the architectural functions of "embodiment" and "admittance." Any environment, thus, *embodies* meanings, at the same time as it *admits* certain actions to take place.

We shall later discuss these functions in more detail, but first we have to take a close look at the two aspects which define our general approach to the analysis of dwelling.

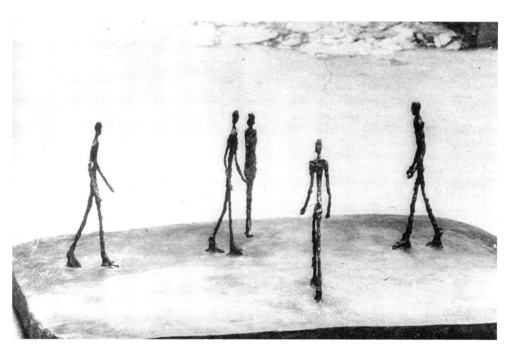

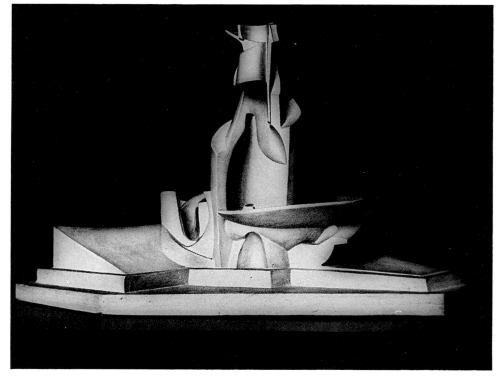

Identification

We have already pointed out that human *identification* means to relate meaningfully to a world of *things*. Our first step, therefore, is to arrive at a definition of the concept of "thing." Today it is common to consider the thing a mere "construct," composed of sensations. What is immediately given, it is asserted, are the sense-data, which constitute things as a result of "experience." This "scientific" approach, however, leads to a dangerous abstraction from concrete reality, and leaves us with a meaningless, relativistic world. A reaction against relativistic atomism is therefore coming to the fore, inspired primarily by phenomenological philosophy. Phenomenology took as its point of departure Husserl's slogan "to the things themselves," and his recognition that modern science did not manage to help our understanding of the concrete "life-world" (*Lebenswelt*).[7] The life-world does not consist of sensations, but is immediately given as a world of characteristic, meaningful things, which do not have to be "constructed" through individual experience. "The thing," Merleau-Ponty says, "is not mediated by our senses, our sensations or our perspectives; we go straight to it, and it is only in a secondary way that we become aware of the limits of our knowledge and of ourselves as knowing."[8] We could also say that man is not born in isolation, but as part of structured totality. Man *has* a world from the very beginning; a world which simply exists. Thus Merleau-Ponty asserts: "...in the interaction of things, each one is characterized by a kind of *a priori* to which it remains faithful... The significance of a thing inhabits that thing...,"[9] and further: "Prior to and independently of other people, the thing achieves that miracle of expression: an inner reality which reveals itself externally...,"[10] and "...expression is the language of the thing itself and springs from its configuration."[11] What, then, *are* these things which reveal their meaning through their configuration? Heidegger offers an answer in a famous essay, where he defines the thing as a "gathering of world."[12] He recalls that the original meaning of the word "thing" is "gathering," and illustrates this significant fact with a phenomenological analysis of a jug. Then he goes on defining the world which is gathered by the thing as a "fourfold" of earth, sky, mortals and divinities, which belong together in a "mirror-play," where "each of the four mirrors is in its own way the essence of the others."[13] In other words, the things are what they are relative to the basic structure of the world. The things make the world appear, and thereby condition man. *Wir sind die Bedingten*, "we are the conditioned (bethinged) ones," Heidegger says. Identification, thus, means to gain a world through the understanding of things. The word "understanding" is here used in the original sense of standing under or among.

If we relate Heidegger's concept of thing to the problem of dwelling, we may say that dwelling primarily consists in the appropriation of a world of things, not in a material sense, but as an ability to interpret the meaning the things gather. "Things visit mortals with a world," Heidegger says, and when we understand their message we gain that existential foothold which is dwelling.

When Heidegger chooses a jug as an illustration, he reaches beyond the things that are given in nature. The jug is man-made, and therefore it is also a *work*. In making a thing such as a jug, man intentionally gathers a world, or in Heidegger's words, "sets a world into work."[14] The twofold nature of dwelling thus appears: first the faculty of understanding the given things (natural or man-made), and second the making of works which keep and "explain" what has been understood. In our context these works are settlement, urban space, institution and house; all of which gather a fourfold world.

An example may illustrate the relationship between world, thing and work. Boccioni's sculpture *Development of a Bottle in Space* (1912) "explains" the "thingness" of the bottle. As a thing, the bottle possesses an inner reality or identity which resides in the world it gathers, and is expressed by its configuration or *Gestalt*. This expression, however, is not immediately intelligible. The bottle stands there, and presents itself as what it is, but somehow its meaning remains hidden. Boccioni's work of art reveals the meaning. It tells us what a bottle *is*, and distinguishes it from other containers such as jug and jar.

The bottle contains a liquid. Simultaneously it encloses and exposes its contents. Even if the bottle is colored, we perceive the volatility of the liquid through the glass; a latent movement is present which together with the reflections in the material make the thing become alive. (An earthenware jar does not possess this life; its character rather resides in its hiding, and in the contrast between material and form and the hidden content.) The lively play in light is kept by the form of the bottle. What is mobile and transient is fixed, and becomes part of the permanent world of things. When the bottle rises in space and *stands*, it conquers inconstancy and gathers multifariousness in a static center. Therefore the bottle has to be symmetrical around the vertical axis and relatively slender; it does not tolerate irregularities. Transparency and reflections, however, create a dynamism which is experienced as an interaction between outside and inside. (In the decanter this effect is emphasized by the facets.) The bottle is therefore simultaneously static and dynamic. The contents give meaning to the bottle as a static-dynamic center.) Water and wine, source and juice, the gift offered to man by earth and sky are gathered and placed in the center, and we gather around. Thus the bottle brings the world close. (A jug cannot in the same way constitute a center; it has a mouth and a handle, it indicates a direction and does not stand at the center of space.)

Boccioni explains the phenomenology of the bottle. In his sculpture a bottle-like figure rises with ordering power out of a complex configuration of straight and curved elements. Without the bottle this configuration would have appeared chaotic. As a gathering center, however, it does not isolate itself within a complete form; rather its faceted contour indicates an active relationship to the surroundings. Hence the bottle "develops" in space, rising out of the transient phenomena as a gathering thing.

In general, Boccioni's bottle tells us that the given things have to be interpreted by man to become an inhabited world. True understanding is made possible by the work of art, which reveals the thingness of things. "Poetry is what really lets us dwell," Heidegger says,[15] and continues: "Poetry does not fly above and surmount the earth in order to escape it and hover over it. Poetry is what first brings man onto the earth, making him belong to it, and thus brings him into dwelling."[16] Works of architecture belong to those poetical revela-

8. *Earth and sky: landscape by J. Ruisdael* (ca. 1670).

9. *Inhabited landscape: winter scene by P. Bruegel* (ca. 1560).

tions which make us dwell. In the following we shall discuss the content of works of architecture, that is, the world they gather, as well as the means which are used to fulfill the gathering, taking the concept of *world* as our point of departure.

So far we have intended "world" as a multitude of distinct, albeit interrelated things. Heidegger's fourfold, however, indicates a more general structure. Thus he uses the categories of *earth* and *sky* to make us see the basic order of things. "Earth is the serving bearer, blossoming and fruiting, spreading out in rock and water, rising up into plant and animal...," he says, and continues: "The sky is the vaulting path of the sun, the course of the changing moon, the wandering glitter of the stars, the year's seasons and their changes, the light and dusk of day, the gloom and glow of night, the clemency and inclemency of the weather, the drifting clouds and the blue depth of the ether."[17] A general and concrete phenomenology of world is here suggested which makes the things become alive as parts of a meaningful whole. Then man enters, and Heidegger says: "If we think of the verb *to dwell* in a wide and essential sense, then it denotes the way in which humans fulfill their wandering from birth to death on earth under the sky. Everywhere the wandering remains the essence of dwelling, as the staying between earth and sky, between birth and death, between joy and pain, between work and world. If we call this multifarious between the *world*, then the world is the house, which is inhabited by the mortals. The single houses, however, the villages, the cities, are works of architecture, which in and around themselves gather the multifarious between. The buildings bring the earth as the inhabited landscape

18

*10. Stimmung: Greifswald in the moonlight
by C. D. Friedrich (1817).*

close to man and at the same time place the nearness of neighborly dwelling under the expanse of the sky."[18]

The world which is gathered by a work of architecture is hence an "inhabited landscape," that is, a landscape which has been "understood" as a particular case of the totality earth-sky, in relation to the four modes of dwelling. The works of architecture, on the various environmental levels, make this understanding a concrete fact. As things, they fulfill their gathering function through their bodily form. In other words, works of architecture are objects of human identification because they *embody* existential meanings, making the world stand forth as it is. How is this embodiment accomplished? Boccioni's bottle already told us that the gathering function of a thing depends on how it "is" in space, that is, how it stands, opens and closes, reflects, etc. Expression, thus, is basically physiognomic, regardless of the nature of the thing, and identification therefore comprises a *rapport* between man's own body and the bodily form of the object. In general, any case of embodiment "mirrors" other things, and represents a certain way of being between earth and sky.

The "between" of earth and sky, however, does not only consist in a complex totality of interrelated things, it also at any moment presents itself as a *Stimmung* or "atmosphere." All landscapes are characterized by an atmosphere which maintains its identity through climatic and seasonal changes. This atmosphere is of essential importance because of its unifying role in the environment, and identification also consists in being open to environmental character. In the past, the particular character or "spirit" of a place was known as the *genius loci*.[19] The genius loci is first of all determined by

a mode of embodiment which is present in most things and works.

Through identification man possesses a world, and thus an identity. Today identity is often considered an "interior" quality of each individual, and growing up is understood as a "realization" of the hidden self. The theory of identification, however, teaches us that identity rather consists in an interiorization of understood things, and that growing up therefore depends on being open to what surrounds us. Although the world is immediately given, it has to be interpreted to be understood, and although man is part of the world, he has to concretize his belonging to feel at home.

Orientation

Identification is never separated from daily life, but always related to our actions. In general, what we are doing depends on the psychological function of *orientation*. We have already pointed out that actions, as a rule, may be understood in terms of goals and paths, which together constitute a field or domain of more or less well-known places. In other words, man acts on the basis of an "environmental image" which is related to the spatial organization of the environment. "A good environmental image gives its possessor an important sense of emotional security," Kevin Lynch says, "which is the obverse of the fear that comes with disorientation."[20] Evidently the image varies with the situation, but it is also possible to work out a general phenomenology of orientation, that is, of existential space.[21] Such a phenomenology aims at defining the meaning of center, path and domain, independently of the circumstantial "content" of the three terms. The goal or *center* is the basic constituent of existential space. Human life is always related to

12. The center as axis mundi: Etruscan tomb.   *13. Path: street in Spoleto.*

21

centers where actions of primary importance take place. Centers are found on all environmental levels; the settlement thus forms a center of arrival in the landscape, the square a center of meeting within the settlement, the institution a center of explanation in the built fabric, and the house a center of personal life. In general, the center represents what is *known*, in contrast to the unknown and perhaps frightening world around. "It is the point where man acquires position in space as a psychic being, the point where he "lingers" and "lives in space," Bollnow says.[22] As a consequence, man has always thought of the whole world as being centered. The ancient Greeks placed the "navel" of the world (*omphalos*) in Delphi, the Romans considered their Capitol the *caput mundi*, and the *Ka'aba* in Mecca is still the center of the Islamic world. In general, "the discovery or projection of a fixed point — the center — is equivalent to the creation of the world," Mircea Eliade says,[23] intending that meaning and center belong together. Centers may be "landmarks" as well as "nodes," to use the terms of Kevin Lynch, and in both cases they appear as conspicuous, imageable "figures," to use a term from Gestalt psychology. We shall later discuss the phenomenology of the center on the different environmental levels. So far we just have to add that the center in general is experienced as a vertical *axis mundi* which unites earth and sky, since it is the point where all horizontal movements come to an end. This is the reason why center and embodied explanation mostly coincide, and why the vertical is considered the *sacred* dimension of space. It represents a "path" towards a reality which may be "higher" or "lower" than daily life, a reality which conquers the gravity of the earth, or succumbs to it. The *axis mundi* is therefore more than a center *on* earth; being a connection between the cosmic realms, it is the place where a breakthrough from one realm to the other can occur. Human life takes place on earth under the sky, and the vertical is therefore experienced as the line of *tension*.

The *path* or axis is a necessary complement to the center, since the latter implies an outside and an inside, or, in other words, the actions of arrival and departure. "An axis is perhaps the first human manifestation," Le Corbusier says, "it is the means of every human act. The toddling child moves along an axis, the man striving in the tempest of life traces for himself an axis."[24] The existential importance of the path is expressed by terms such as "parting of the ways," "stand in one's way," and "on the right way." Paths are present on all environmental levels, and in general represent a *possibility* of movement, in contrast to the experience of getting "lost."[25] Directions are also an intrinsic property of the world, as is shown by the qualitative differences ascribed to north, south, east and west by various cultures. The cardinal points thus become a referential system of orientation. In some cases directions are a principal symbol of man's being-in-the-world, such as the Egyptian way, the Roman pair of crossing axes (*cardo-decumanus*) and the Chrisitan *via crucis*. We shall later discuss the phenomenology of the path on the different environmental levels. So far, we just have to add that the horizontal path in general represents man's concrete world of action, and that the directions taken together form a plane of infinite extension. On this plane man chooses and creates paths which give his existential space a particular structure. Sometimes the path

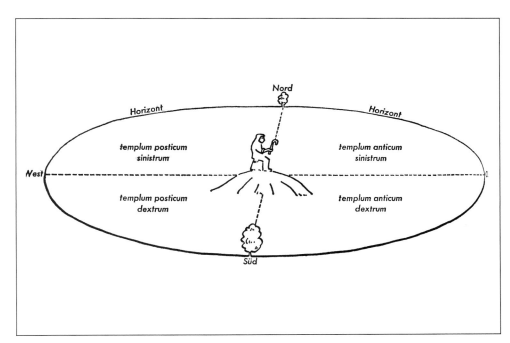

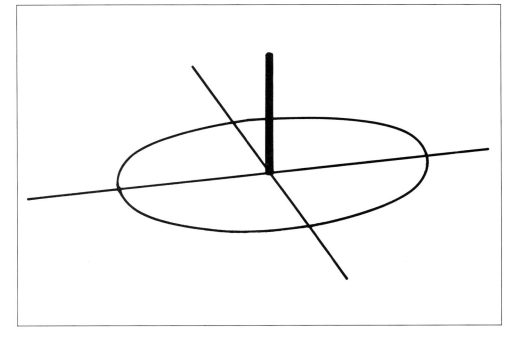

leads to a known goal, but often it only indicates an intended direction, gradually dissolving into the unknown distance. A path is in general determined by its "continuity," to use another Gestalt term. In any case, the movement along a path is distinguished by a certain *rhythm*, which forms a complement to the tension connected with the vertical. Tension and rhythm, thus, are general properties of man's orientation in the world.

The figural quality of centers and paths implies a less structured "ground" on which they stand forth. Man's environmental image thus comprises more or less extended *domains* which are distinguished by a certain qualitative uniformity. We orientate within and in relation to these domains, which have a unifying function in existential space. They fill out the network of paths and make it become a "space." If we think of our own country, or the earth as a whole, we primarily think of domains: fields, lakes, deserts, mountains and oceans, which form a continuous mosaic. Because of their general properties, domains function as potential places for man's actions. Orientation, therefore, implies structuring the environment into domains by means of paths and centers. The Roman settlement may serve as an example. Its pair of axes not only defined the cardinal points, but also divided the area into four domains or "quarters." City districts are in fact still called quarters. From ancient times the world was imagined as consisting of four parts, and the Roman city hence acted as an *imago mundi*. The rituals performed during the foundation of a Roman settlement, demonstrate that the purpose was to define a comprehensive spatial order related to a primary center.[26] This order was established within the *finalis circulus* or horizon,

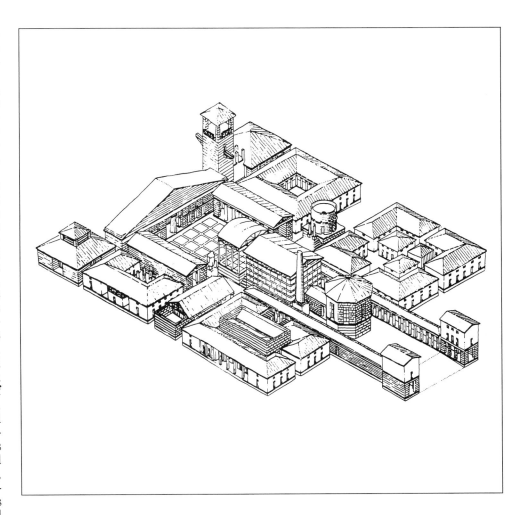

which thus becomes another fundamental element of orientation. The constituent elements of a domain obviously possess tensions and rhythms, but as such the domain is distinguished by a *Stimmung* or "atmosphere." We have already pointed out that the atmosphere is a general object of identification, and understand that orientation within the domain it belongs to, completes man's being-in-the-world.

Our discussion of human orientation shows that having a world does not only mean identification with the qualities embodied by things, but also orientation within the space they constitute. Space *admits* actions, and hence allows life to take place. As a "between" of earth and sky, however, existential space is basically different from mathematical space. Its centers and directions are qualitatively determined, and as a consequence it is heterogeneous rather than isotropic. The setting-into-work of existential space is therefore not a simple question of applied geometry. The concept of orientation offers a key to the problem, just as the study of identification told us how a building may embody existential meanings. Whereas embodiment is determined by how an architectural form stands, rises, opens and closes, admittance depends on spatial organization in terms of centers, paths and domains. On all environmental levels works of architecture have to possess a spatial order of this kind, which is related to the given natural space as well as the patterns of human action.

Buildings, therefore, do not only gather the "multifarious between" because of their built form, but also because they visualize the spatial properties of a situation. Any case of admittance thus represents a certain way of being between earth and sky.

The language of architecture

The architectural means which are employed to make man's being-in-the-world an accomplished fact, are in general embodiment and admittance, or, in architectural terms, built form and organized space. We have asserted that built form and organized space possess general properties, which become manifest on the various environmental levels. The general properties do not exist in a concrete sense, but only as expressive possibilities which have to be set into work as settlement, urban space, institution and house. The single work, however, is also a case of a general category which, as such, does not "exist." The categories of works of architecture are usually known as building *types*, a term which applies to large totalities (e.g. settlement and urban space) as well as elements of a more limited size (e.g. individual buildings and their parts). Together built form, organized space and building types cover the aspects and modes of dwelling, and thus constitute a "language" of means which may satisfy the need for gathering the "multifarious between." We may call the study of the three interdependent constituents of the language of architecture *morphology*, *topology* and *typology*.[27]

Morphology is concerned with the "how" of built form, and in the single work of architecture is concretized as "formal articulation." It follows from what has been said above, that built forms are always understood in terms of their being between earth and sky, that is, their standing, rising and opening. The word "stand" denotes the relationship to the earth, "rise" the relationship to the sky, and "open" refers to the interaction with the environment, that is, the relationship between outside and inside. Standing is

20. The setting-into-work of standing:
the Hephaisteion in Athens (450-440 B.C.).

21. The setting-into-work of opening: house
at the Baleares by J. Utzon.

embodied through the treatment of the base and wall. A massive and perhaps concave base ties the building to the ground, whereas an emphasis on the vertical direction tends to make it "free." Verticality, rising lines, and certain forms such as a serrate silhouette, express an active relationship to the sky and a wish for receiving light. The outside-inside relationship is first of all expressed through the treatment of the openings in the wall. In the wall, thus, earth and sky meet, and the way man "is" on earth is embodied in this meeting. But the meeting of earth and sky is not only made manifest by vertical tensions. "Earth" and "sky" also imply concrete properties such as material texture, color and light. In general, morphology studies the concrete structure of floor, wall and roof (ceiling), or, in short, the spatial *boundaries*. The character of a form is determined by its boundaries. Thus Heidegger says: "A boundary is not that at which something stops but, as the Greeks recognized, the boundary is that from which something begins its presencing."[28]

Topology is concerned with spatial order, and is in the single work of architecture concretized as "spatial organization." The term "topology" is chosen to indicate that architectural space derives from place (Greek: *topos*) rather than abstract mathematical space. We have already discussed the basic constituents of organized space: center, path and domain, and should only add that together they form the simple structure of a horizontal plane subdivided by paths, delimited by a horizon and pierced by a vertical axis.[29] On the various environmental levels this structure may be more or less clearly expressed, and repeated with variations to form complex totalities. In some cases the structural

elements do not possess a defined geometrical form, but are merely "topologically" determined, that is, in terms of proximity, continuity and closure,[30] making thus a somewhat vague understanding of the environment manifest. When the elements get a geometrically precise form, however, they become the expression of a more clearly conceived environmental organization, abstracted from nature or imposed by man.

A basic property of existential space is the distinction between horizontal and vertical, and accordingly the two directions play a constituent role within the language of architecture.[31] The horizontal relates to the earth and the vertical to the sky, and thus they determine the kind of dwelling which a certain work of architecture makes manifest. To become manifest, however, horizontal and vertical have to be *built*. Thus they are the common denominator which unite organized space and built form and give the work of architecture its figurative identity, as a certain way of being-in-the-world. *Typology*, finally, is concerned with the manifestations of the modes of dwelling. The very word indicates that places are not an endless multitude of basically different cases, but constitute a universe of meaningful identities. The broad categories of settlement, urban space, institution and house already illustrate this fact, but we may also carry typological differentiation further and talk about "tower" and "hall," "dome" and "gable," etc. In the single work the type becomes manifest as an image or *figure*. The language of architecture thus comprises *archetypes* on all environmental levels. The archetypes may be defined as modes of dwelling concretized by means of the general principles of embodiment and spatial organization.[32]

The types are the essences of architecture, corresponding to the names of spoken language. Names belong to things, and thus designate the content of our everyday life-world. The world, in fact, is not only given as a world of things but also as a universe of names. "Language is the house of Being," Heidegger says.[33] Language therefore does not only serve as communication, but discloses the basic existential structures. The archetypes hence disclose basic life situations. Man's being-in-the-world is structured, and the structure is kept and visualized by means of architecture. Evidently a work of architecture does not make a total world visible, but only certain of its aspects, which are indicated by the concept of "inhabited landscape." As such the typological entities represent what is general, whereas the individual work, as a variation on the typological theme, makes a circumstantial adaptation manifest.

Setting-into-work
Setting-into-work is a twofold process. First, it means that a mode of dwelling is translated into a typological entity by means of the basic principles of built form and organized space, and second, that this type is modified in accordance with the circumstances of the here and now. The first step constitutes the language of architecture, whereas the second makes it "speak." Thus Louis Kahn says: "A work of architecture is an offering to Architecture," intending that the work is made possible by the language of architecture. When the language is used to express the actual circumstances, what is general is related to what is local and temporal. General are the basic facts of morphology, topology and typology, local and temporal the given environment and the actual building task.

Language as such is timeless and placeless, although it contains the original "memories" of mankind. Life, however, takes place in time, and demands our understanding and participation. It is complex and transient, and would remain meaningless and intolerable, if it were not related to what is general. To live is to resist transience and to "bury the seed-corn in the ground." This does not imply that the course of time has to be stopped, rather it means that the moment is interpreted as a case of the timeless.

It is also a well-known fact, however, that history cannot be understood as a succession of moments. History consists of "epochs" and "traditions," that is, of relative constancies within transient time. To some extent these constancies may be explained as a result of the *stabilitas loci*. Since places do not change continuously, local adaptation remains basically similar during long periods. Constancies, however, are also due to *memory*. Beyond the original memories preserved in language, any tradition comprises more particular memories which become manifest as a "style," that is, a particular set of forms. In general, memories are always records of the "multifarious between," as the Greeks realized when they understood the goddess *Mnemosyne*, "memory," as the daughter of Earth and Sky. Being the mother of the muses, memory gives rise to art, and, in fact, art serves to remember what is general at every passing moment, giving thereby meaning to life here and now.

As a local and temporal interpretation of the timeless, setting-into-work implies a modification of the archetypes. Being exposed to circumstantial "forces," they change without losing their identity. The process is beautifully illustrated by the diffusion of the *clas-*

sical language of architecture. "Modification," however, also implies combination and interaction. As a gathering thing, the work of architecture might unify several archetypes to form a new kind of synthesis. Simple or complex, the work always possesses the quality of image or figure. "Poetry speaks in images," Heidegger says, and "the nature of the image is to let something be seen."[34] The word "figure" suggests that the architectural image appears as a concrete shape or volume, and that it therefore belongs to the category of things. A figure possesses concrete presence and participates in the constitution of the environment. We could also say that the figures represent a reconquest of the lost archetypes, and bring permanence into movement and change. The meaning of a work of architecture therefore consists in its gathering the world in a general typical sense, in a local particular sense, in a temporal historical sense, and, finally, *as something*, that is, as the figural manifestation of a mode of dwelling between earth and sky. A work of architecture does not exist in a vacuum, but in the world of things and human beings, and reveals this world as what it is. Thus it helps man to *dwell poetically*. Man dwells poetically when he is able to "listen" to the saying of things, and when he is capable of setting what he apprehends into work by means of the language of architecture.

II. Settlement

To settle in the landscape means to delimit an area, a place. We stop our wandering and say: *Here!* Then we create an "inside" within the encompassing "outside." The settlement is therefore a point of *arrival*.[35] Still we may somewhere have the fine experience of approaching a settlement which waits for us like a "thing." First we grasp the main outline and perhaps a dominant element, such as a steeple. Getting closer, the shape becomes more articulate, and begins to suggest something about what is hidden inside. Depending on where we come from, the experience varies. If we come through the forest it is different from coming across the fields or over the sea; but always we have the sense of having reached a goal. Like a magnet it attracts us, and arouses our expectations.

How, then, does a settlement become a goal? The very experience of arrival implies a relationship to what is left behind. A goal does not exist in a vacuum; it is only a goal in relation to its environment. We have already suggested that this relation consists in its "gathering" the surrounding world. Thus the settlement acts as a *center* and invites man to dwell. At a center we shall not feel that we are in a *different* place, but where the environment is "explained." Somebody who has his personal dwelling out in the countryside should not feel a foreigner when visiting the center, but rather experience that his own place becomes part of a larger whole.

A settlement may gather a more or less comprehensive world. The farm and the village are related to their immediate surroundings (although these usually belong to a larger region), whereas the town has a wider frame of reference. The capital city, finally, ought to function as a gathering center to a whole country. In general, the problem is to settle in such a way that a "friendly" relationship with the site is established. Such a friendship implies that man respects and takes *care* of the given place. Taking care, however, does not mean to leave things as they are; rather they ought to be revealed and cultivated. Thus the settlement interprets the site and transforms it into a place where human life may take place.

Every landscape has a certain character and spatial structure which are denoted by names. Thus we say: "valley," "basin" and "plain"; that is, spaces which vary with the topography and the presence of rocks, vegetation and water. The orientation is also important, as it relates the site to natural light and to a particular microclimate. Landscapes possess a varying degree of complexity, comprising subordinate localities with a distinct character. In the past such differences determined the localization of sanctuaries which represented the natural "forces."[36] Particularly significant are the centers suggested by the landscape itself, that is, those places where the world so to speak gathers itself. Natural centers obviously play a decisive role in determining the choice of a "here" for human settlement, and therefore ought to be given some attention.

What properties, then, distinguish a natural center? In general we may say that the natural center is a place where earth and sky are interrelated to form a conspicuous totality. This happens in three characteristic ways. First, the earth may rise up towards the sky to form a peak or ridge. The "high place," thus, has always been preferred by man, not only because it gives a sense of being closer to heaven, but because it offers the possibility to overlook the surrounding world. Thus it gives a con-

vincing sense of being at the center. Second, the earth may "receive" the sky by receding to form a basin or valley. Such depressions are usually more fertile than the surrounding land and therefore indicate the presence of the sky as a fertilizing agent. A basin is furthermore surrounded by an elevated horizon which endows the sky with the quality of a regular dome. Finally, the earth may reflect the sky and blend with it. This happens when the ground contains a circumscribed water surface, such as a pond, lake or bay. The lake gathers the world in a catoptric image, which, since it stands upside-down, reveals the general atmosphere of the place rather than its constituent things. The image, however, is not flat, but comprises the height of the sky as well as the depth of the earth. The explanation it offers is therefore unfathomable, and the world appears as a place of simultaneous revelation and concealment. No wonder, hence, that man always experienced lakes and bays as significant goals, where he could find rest from his wandering.

When a natural center is used for the localization of a settlement, architecture serves to reveal and emphasize qualities that are already present. We call this process *visualization*.[37] Buildings, thus, may give emphasis to a peak or a ridge, as is illustrated by innumerable Italian hill-towns. Or they may form a center to a basin, or a point of arrest to the movement of a valley (often together with a bridge which connects its two sides). Or, finally, buildings may follow the delimitation of a lake or a bay and offer points of observation, from where the mirror-play or earth and sky may be experienced.

When a natural center is not present, as in the desert or on an extended

23. Arrival: Palombara Sabina in Latium.

plain, architecture has to add what is lacking. We call this process *complementation*. That is, buildings are used to define an area, and establish a relationship between earth and sky. Desert architecture in fact consists of two conspicuous elements: the perimetral wall which gives halt to infinite extension, and the slender vertical (e.g. the minaret) which is simultaneously center and *axis mundi*. In both cases the transformation of the site into a place for dwelling is achieved by means of built form and organized space, and we have to consider both aspects in some detail in order to understand the nature of the settlement. As a point of departure for the discussion, we shall take the experience of *arrival*.

To serve as a goal, a settlement has to possess *figural* quality in relation to the surrounding landscape. It is this quality that makes it possible to call the settlement a "place." A group of buildings only appears as a figure if it is relatively dense, or has a clear delimitation. The city walls of the past therefore did not only serve fortificatory purposes, but contributed essentially to the identity of the place. If buildings are scattered around, this identity is lost, at the same time as the continuous ground of the landscape is destroyed. Figural quality, however, changes somewhat according to the local topographical conditions. In a grand landscape large units of buildings are more natural than where the environment possesses a varied "microstructure." In general, figural quality depends on built form *and* organized space.

Morphology

When we approach a settlement, the skyline is usually of decisive importance. What we perceive is a figure

which rises from the ground towards the sky in a certain way. It is this standing and rising which determines our expectations and tells us where we are. Thus the settlement presents itself as a particular local *character* which visualizes and complements the environment. When we travel through a landscape, we are "tuned" in a certain way, and the settlement ought to offer an answer to our expectations. Since the effect of the landscape is determined by its gathering of earth and sky, the settlement must make an analogous relationship manifest. Thus it appears as a condensation, and hence an explanation of the local character. We could also say that it serves as a focal point where the dispersed properties of the surroundings are gathered. The settlement fills this role through its standing and rising, and primarily through its most conspicuous overall property: the *silhouette*.

In the old city atlases the places are always presented in elevation and plan, or in our terms, as built form and organized space. The elevation appears more frequently, as it most directly reveals the character of the settlement. (The word "elevation" in fact designates how something rises above the ground). Matthaeus Merian's *Topographies* from about 1650 offer abundant examples.[38] In some cases, such as Istanbul or Prague, the skyline as a whole may be the object of our identification because of the intimate rapport between topography and built form. More often, however, the local character is determined by prominent vertical elements which stand forth from the main form. Towers and domes, thus, are the primary "figures" which represent a settlement in relation to its surroundings. We may remind of famous cases such as the dome of St. Peter's in Rome, the steeple

34

of St. Stephen's in Vienna, the Eiffel Tower in Paris and the cluster of skyscrapers in Lower Manhattan to corroborate this fact. Even when the general figural quality of a settlement is lost, as is the case in most cities today, a tower may represent the place and make human identification and orientation possible.

Any tower (or dome) embodies a certain way of being between earth and sky, and it does this by defining a man-made center. Thus it brings the "inhabited landscape" close to man. This happens in a twofold way. When the settlement is seen from afar, the tower gathers the surroundings, at the same time as it signals what is hidden inside. When we have entered, the tower reminds us of the environment, at the same time as it forms a focus to the built habitat. The tower, thus, acts as a unifying link between inside and outside and expresses the basic quality of being in a certain place.

The morphology of the tower has, to our knowledge, never been studied.[39] We cannot therefore present any detailed account, but only remind of such characteristic examples as the infinitely varied steeples of the nordic countries, the classical *campanili* of Northern Italy, the sculptural Baroque helms of Central Europe, the picturesque onion domes of Russia, and the various kinds of needle-like Islamic minarets. Local, cultural and historical values are gathered by these forms, and always *as something*, that is, as the tower of a church, a town hall, a castle, a city wall, or even as a "tower-house."[40] In historical cities several of these elements may be simultaneously present, forming thus a fascinating ensemble of expressive landmarks. Sometimes the towers are visually related to other vertical shapes, such as pointed gables, and appear, even when

27. *Figural quality and silhouette: Lübeck in a painting by H. Rode (1482).*

28. *Istanbul, city of silhouettes: "veduta" by M. Merian (ca. 1650).*

seen from a distance, as a particularly prominent variation on a common, local theme.

The morphology of the dome is both related to and different from that of the tower. What they have in common, is their being vertical elements which stand up in space and therefore mark a center. Whereas the tower, however, appears as a compact mass, the dome is experienced as a volume which contains an interior. The dome therefore does not only define a center, but also acts as a condensed image of the surrounding world. No wonder, hence, that the dome is at home in the classical South, where the total environment is spontaneously perceived as an encompassing dome-like space. By means of surface articulation, however, its standing up may be variously interpreted, and different relationships between earth and sky thus defined. The fundamental possibilities are evidently the expression of rising actively in space (e.g. numerous Baroque domes), or being harmoniously at rest (e.g. Renaissance domes), or appearing as if it is lowered down from above (e.g. certain late-Byzantine domes).

By acting both as an exterior and an interior form, the dome does not only determine the silhouette of a settlement, but also constitutes a primary goal to urban space. When seen from afar, the dome of St. Peter's in Rome signals the presence of something which arouses our expectations and directs our movement. Upon approach, it hides itself behind Maderno's nave, but is again revealed in its interior aspect when we enter the church. Our expectations are thus satisfied by an "explanation" of the previously experienced exterior form.

The general meaning of a settlement is revealed by its silhouette. This basic fact is particularly well illustrated by

32. *The minarets of the Blue Mosque, Istanbul.*
33. *The Damascus Gate, Jerusalem.*
34. *Russian "onion" domes, Kishi (1764).*

35. Jerusalem in a view by D. Roberts (1839).

the old city of Jerusalem, where the multifarious "contents" are signalled to the surrounding world by characteristic turrets and domes. Thus we find minarets, classical *campanili*, Byzantine cupolas and even Russian onions forming a meaningful symbiosis, with the golden Dome of the Rock as a primary gathering center. Better than in most other places we here experience the possibilities of visualizing the relationship of earth and sky and man's being in the "between." Thanks to the powerful engirdling city-wall, a general figural unity is however secured. The life of the city through the historical epochs also becomes manifest in its masonry, from the incredibly powerful blocks of the Jewish-Herodian substructure to the "abstract" linearity of the Islamic-Osmanian elevations. At the main openings in the wall, namely the Damascus Gate, the skyline of the place is condensed into a picturesque succession of varied merlons. The different existential interpretations gathered by Jerusalem are also unified by the use of the same building material throughout. Even today it is required that the local white-golden stone should be employed in all buildings, and as a result the various symbolic forms become "rooted" in the locality. A simple, but efficient and meaningful way of making a "here" become manifest. In general, the example of Jerusalem shows that the overall built form of a settlement interprets the site in relation to chosen socio-cultural values. Thus it embodies located human togetherness.

Topology

Human togetherness implies that life is admitted to take place by means of an appropriate spatial organization. The figural character of a settlement, thus, is not only determined by its delimitation and by the single elements that constitute its skyline, but also by the way the elements are grouped. Evidently the grouping is conditioned from without and from within, that is, by the configuration of the given site as well as the social structure of the fellowship.

A study of settlement patterns demonstrates that the infinitely many individual places may be understood as variations on a few basic types of spatial organization. In general we may distinguish between three types: the *cluster*, the *row* and the *enclosure*. The cluster consists of elements (buildings) which are organized by means of simple proximity, without possessing any kind of geometrical order or symmetry. In the row they are placed along a continuous line, whose curvature remains "free." In the enclosure, finally, the elements form a closed figure around a space. Wherever we go in the world, we encounter these forms, which determine the layout of farms, villages and towns.[41]

When we say that the spatial organization is conditioned by the configuration of the site, it does not mean that there exists a one-to-one correspondence. A valley or crest may suggest a row structure and a basin an engirdling enclosure, but a certain freedom of interpretation is always present, according to the need for visualization or complementation. In any case, however, the basic aim is to establish a meaningful relationship between the configuration of the site and the spatiality of the human fellowship.

This aim is facilitated by the fact that the basic settlement patterns follow the Gestalt laws of organization. We could also say that man perceives and organizes according to the same principles, which we have already recognized as "proximity," "continuity" and "closure," with "similarity" as a more general category.[42] Piaget's studies of the child's conception of space arrive at analogous conclusions. In general, Piaget characterizes the basic forms of organization as *topological*, to distinguish them from the more precise *geometrical* conceptions which develop somewhat later in life. The geometrical conceptions, however, are not essentially different from the topological ones, rather they represent an interpretation of these. The cluster, thus, becomes a regular group or grid, the row an axis, and the enclosure a circle or polygon.[43]

Within a topological pattern the elements maintain a certain individual freedom, whereas the geometrical layout implies a dominant, superior order. A given site hardly asks for such an order; natural spatiality is as a rule topological, and its visualization by means of built forms usually produces a counterpoint of topological patterns. An exception is offered by the unique spatial structure of Egypt, where the regular course of the Nile suggests a north-south axis crossed at a right angle by the east-west path of the sun. As a result, Egyptian settlements (town, necropolis, temple) show a strictly geometrical organization.[44] We have also referred to the geometrical layout of the Roman city, which does not take a particular geographical situation as its point of departure, but the basic structure of the sky. Any geometrical pattern of this kind aims at revealing a general order inherent in the world, in contrast to the topological nature of the individual place. Vernacular settlements from all parts of the world are in fact topologically organized, and thus express the primary importance of the site, with which man has to come to terms.

Why, then, do we encounter so many

41

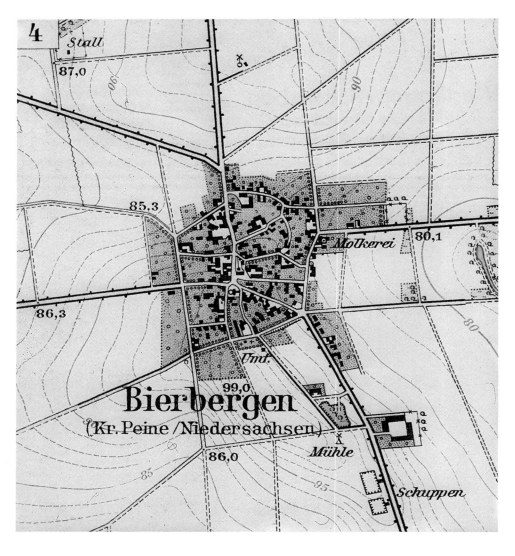

geometrical layouts during architectural history? The reason is evidently that a certain "agreement" was imposed upon the situation. A geometrical pattern implies clearly defined centers and paths, and thus a shared form of life. What is thereby lost, is the basic form of meeting; collective togetherness becomes public order, and the settlement the expression of an accomplished choice. Such a choice, however, is usually not arbitrary, but represents an understood world, where nature as well as man are comprised. In general we may say that the settlement lives in the tension between meeting as simple togetherness and meeting as chosen or imposed agreement. Since both aspects are fundamental existential structures, any settlement ought to comprise topological as well as geometrical forms of spatial organization. In fact, most historical cities did, although the mutual relationship has varied considerably, from the basically topological layout of the Greek *polis*, to the dominant geometrical system of the Roman *civitas*.

Jerusalem may again be mentioned as an interesting example of the combination of topology and geometry. As a whole, the city is a dense, topological cluster which expresses the coming together of people from "all" directions. The movement of the perimetral wall, however, suggests an overall, albeit irregular, square shape. Within this shape two main thoroughfares divide the area into four domains or quarters, which are inhabited by different groups: Jews, Moslems, Christians and Armenians. The thoroughfares originated in the topography of the land, and were after 70 A.D. given emphasis by the Roman conquerors as the axes of *cardo* and *decumanus*.[45] The geometry of quarters endows

37. *Row village in Germany (Reihendorf).* 38. *Round village in Germany (Rundling).*

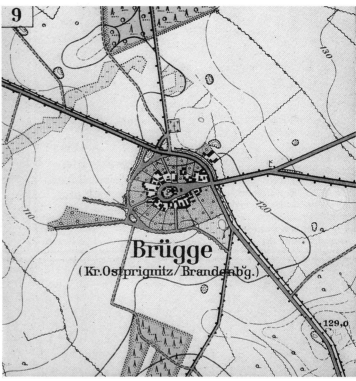

the meeting-place with a significant meaning. Different "worlds" are thus brought together in relation to the cardinal points: the Jewish world which gained its identity when the "chosen people" wandered through the barren, mountainous South, the Islamic world which originated in the infinite deserts of the East, and the Christian world which is rooted in the fertile northern land of Galilee. The Armenian quarter, finally, represents an echo of the more distant worlds which have been conditioned by the message of Jerusalem. Thus the organized space of the city admits the life of a complex totality, interrelating its constituent parts to form a comprehensive place. The dimensions of nature, the modes of human dwelling and the vicissitudes of history are all gathered by the form of this unique city, which therefore especially well illustrates the nature of the human settlement.

Whereas the figural properties of a built form are spontaneously perceived, the spatial organization of a complex organism demands a closer acquaintance with the place. As has been demonstrated by Kevin Lynch, it is essential, however, that we develop an image of the settlement as a whole. We may conclude that such an image-making presupposes the presence of a topologically or geometrically organized space, or, in other words, of imageable spatial figures.

Topology

The figural quality of the settlement consists in two interrelated properties: a "thing"-like built form and a space organized in terms of centers, paths and domains. The interrelation between the two aspects is obvious: the built form gives character to the spatial elements, at the same time as the latter are constituted by the former. To-

41. *"Lamentation of Christ," detail (A. Dürer, 1500.)*

gether, built form and organized space make up a *place*, on a certain environmental level. The comprehensive level of "settlement," thus, comprises several sub-levels, which are known as "farm," "village," "town" and "city."[46] Today, the typology of settlements is generally studied exclusively in terms of spatial organization, an approach which misses their concrete figural quality. In the past, however, places were understood as "things," possessing general as well as individual characteristics. Thus they were recognized as objects of human identification, or as dwelling-places, in the true sense of the word. This fact is clearly revealed by the *vedute* which illustrate the old topographies.[47] The above-mentioned books of Merian offer an abundance of examples, but we may also remind of the famous prints of Piranesi as well as the representations of farms, villages and towns in the works of painters from many countries.

In general, the *veduta* aimed at grasping the essence of the place and fixing its quality in one characteristic image. The choice of standpoint is therefore decisive, and the selection of those elements which constitute our memory of a certain place. We have already mentioned Merian's famous views of Constantinople and Prague. The former shows the city seen from Galata across the Golden Horn. Thus it appears as an extended skyline along the crest of the promontory on which the habitat is located. The natural site and the built form are unified in one unforgettable image which brings forth Constantinople's basic character as a "city of silhouettes." Prague is also shown in relation to the landscape, being situated on the flat land within the bend of the river Vltava under the steep castle hill on the other side of the

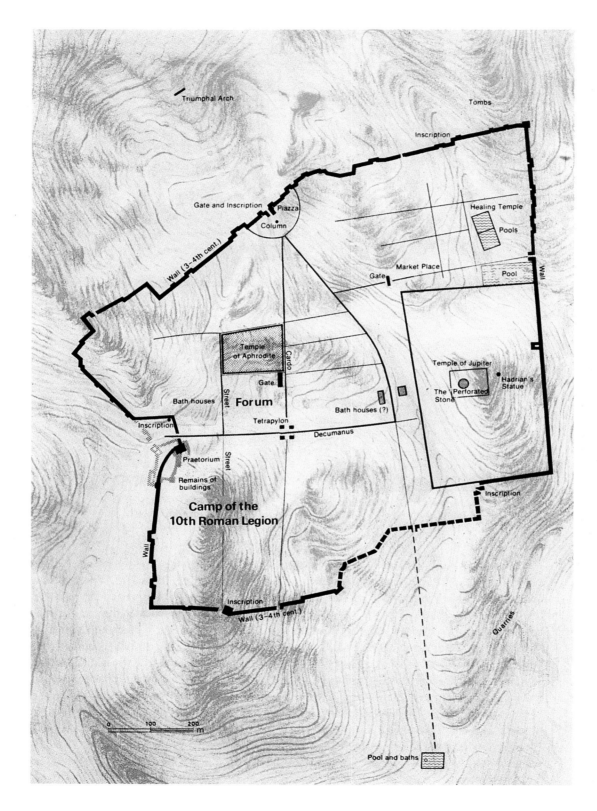

Triumphal Arch

Tombs

Inscription

Gate and Inscription — Piazza
Column

Healing Temple

Pools

Wall (3–4th cent.)

Gate — Market Place

Pool

Wall

Temple
of Aphrodite

Cardo

Temple of Jupiter

Gate

Hadrian's
Statue

Bath houses

Forum

Street

Bath houses (?)

The Perforated
Stone

Inscription

Tetrapylon

Decumanus

Praetorium

Remains of
buildings

Inscription

**Camp of the
10th Roman Legion**

Wall

Quarries

Inscription

Wall (3–4th cent.)

0   100   200
m

Pool and baths

bridge. In Kafka's *Castle* this image is recalled in the very first sentences: "It was late in the evening when K. arrived. The village was deep in snow. The castle hill was hidden, veiled in mist and darkness, nor was there even a glimmer of light to show that a castle was there. On the wooden bridge leading from the main road to the village K. stood for a long time gazing into the illusory emptiness above him." Here the *imago loci* is indicated as one of the basic dimensions of the "life" of the novel. Jerusalem is also one of those cities whose identity may be represented in a single *veduta*. In David Roberts' view from the Mount of Olives (1839), Jerusalem appears as what it "is": a plateau-settlement surrounded by deep ravines and barren hills, containing a multitude of symbolic landmarks, with the Dome of the Rock as a gathering "cosmic" center. An understood world is revealed by the built figure and fixed in our memory in the unique image.

The examples demonstrate that the identity of a settlement consists in basic figural properties, where the word "figural" is not intended in abstract spatial terms, but as a composition of concrete thing-like elements. We may describe such properties, saying for instance: "along the river," "around the market," "on the plateau," "under the hill." The inexhaustible fascination of a city such as Prague consists in a multitude of such relationships, which however unify to form one conspicuous image.

Many place-names denote general types which become manifest as different environmental characters according to the given situation. Thus we find "fords" and "ports" in the North as well as in the South. The variations may, however, be classified in certain broad categories, which the present

writer has defined as "classical," "romantic" and "cosmic."[48] Since these terms are introduced to denote general environmental qualities, they unify natural and human properties. The images of towns which appear in so many paintings of the Renaissance, well illustrate the difference between classical and romantic interpretations of the same kind of settlement. Ambrogio Lorenzetti's *City on the Sea* (Siena, Pinacoteca) is basically classical in approach, although it contains Gothic details. All the buildings are constituted by simple, geometric volumes, and the city wall with its gates and towers and the buildings within all belong to the same figural family. We may make a comparison with the city shown in the background of Dürer's *Lamentation of Christ* (Munich, Alte Pinakotek) where steep roofs and pointed shapes emphasize the "Romantic," expressionist character of the whole. The basic forms of arrival and togetherness are in these examples related to different natural worlds, and the result are places with a distinct figural quality. A further illustration is offered by the frequent representations of towns in Russian icons. A border scene from the St. Nicholas of Zaraisk icon (Novgorod, Museum) shows the characteristic Russian perimetral wall which contrasts with the picturesque multitude of arches and cupolas within. In all three cases, thus, we have conspicuous images which "keep" the local character of a settlement.

Since historical towns usually have particularly distinguished locations, they tend to possess a more pronounced individuality than villages and farms. The towns therefore do not only constitute a practical network, but also reveal the various *qualities* of a country, and function as centers of human identification. Villages, on the contrary, visualize the general character of a region, and are "homes" rather than focal points. In Germany, thus, their names often have endings such as *heim, hausen* or *hofen*. What villages and towns always had in common was the figural quality which is the condition of any "here."

A particularly interesting problem is how a settlement may preserve its identity during the course of time. Although social conditions and artistic styles have changed, many important centers have remained the "same" throughout history. Evidently this is due to the fact that the works of the various epochs may be understood as interpretations of a stable *genius loci*.[49] The problem of temporal continuity is well illustrated by the "eternal city" Rome, where the configuration of the land and the local mode of building has conditioned the character of the habitat from Italic times till the present day.[50]

Again we see, thus, that the given space and form, as a particular relationship of earth and sky, determine the identity of the place. What man does when he builds, is to reveal and interpret what is already there. Thus he takes care of the earth and establishes a friendly relation to the landscape. To take care of the earth therefore does not only mean to cultivate the soil, but to settle in such a way that the earth is revealed as what it is. The act of settling is always collective, but the settlement is not a mere "expression" of society. Rather it shows how a fellowship has understood the given environment where its life takes place, and been able to set this understanding into work *as a settlement*, that is, as a built spatial form which brings the inhabited landscape close. The figural quality is the manifestation of the solution of this problem. Our discussion has shown that the figural quality of settlements may be typologically described, and analyzed in terms of built form and organized space. In general we may say that the figural quality of the settlement allows for natural dwelling.

Settlement today

Our exposition of the morphology, topology and typology of the settlement may seem to be of mere historical interest. Today settlements do not have walls and gates any more, and only rarely they appear as "figures" in the landscape. Their skyline is not distinguished by symbolic forms such as towers and domes, but rather by highrise office buildings which hardly embody any deeper understanding of the world. The modern city, in fact, has for several decades been conceived in terms which are contrary to those outlined above. Thus it has been defined as a "green" spatial continuum into which large separate buildings are placed. The aim behind this conception was the reconquest of the "elementary joys": light, air and green.[51] The loss of the traditional settlement, and hence the *loss of place*, is therefore not an unexpected consequence of a new way of life, but the result of conscious theories of planning. At the present moment, however, we experience a growing reaction against the green city. It does not offer any sense of *arrival*, and has become a "nowhere," which, because of its dispersed built fabric, destroys the landscape rather than bringing it close. Thus we do not only lose the gathering center, but also its world. In general it is becoming ever more evident that the loss of the figurally defined settlement has brought about a weakened sense of human belonging and thus a dangerous loss of identity. What a few years ago might have seemed pure unrealistic nostalgia, has therefore become an actual aim: dense,

44. Project for Echternach by L. Krier (1970).

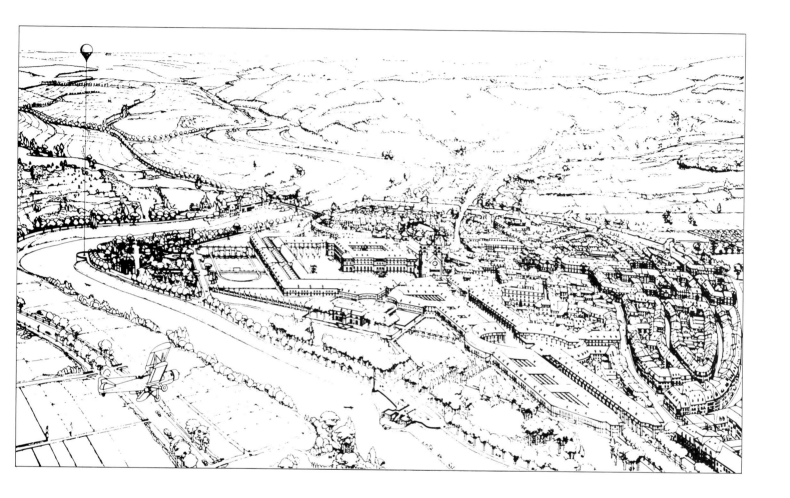

clearly delimited settlements are again appearing, and the need for a reconquest of the figural quality is strongly felt. Kevin Lynch's insistence on the importance of "edges" and "landmarks" is symptomatic of the new attitude. The abstract kind of planning which dominated the scene after the Second World War is hence being substituted by a more concrete approach. It is therefore not surprising that the *veduta* is back as a means of representing the identity of a settlement, as is demonstrated by Leon Krier's birds-eye view of Echternach (1970). An authentic recovery of the settlement presupposes an understanding of the *genius loci* and of the basic typologies in terms of built form and organized space. Today, however, a formalistic approach is *en vogue*, which takes geometrical patterns as the point of departure in combination with borrowed conventional motifs.[52] Let us remind of the topological nature of the settlement as a manifestation of the spatiality of a fellowship in relation to a given site. In a pluralistic epoch like ours, it is even more important to preserve topological freedom than it was in the past. So far modern architecture interpreted freedom in terms of the *plan libre*, transferring a concept which might be valid on the environmental level of the house to the level of the settlement. As a result, the settlement disappeared. What we need today is another kind of freedom which understands the settlement as a coming together of diversities, albeit with the respect for the shared *genius loci* as a common denominator.

Meeting

When we enter the settlement and say "here," a world of possibilities is opened up. Our choice has still to be made, but the world which is here gathered, inspires our desires and asks for a decision. Let us remind of Kahn's words: "A city is a place where a small boy, as he walks through it, may see something that will tell him what he wants to do his whole life."[53] The city, thus, is the place where *meeting* takes place. Here men come together to discover the world of the others. "I am" becomes like a mirror which receives, reflects and presents. In the city all things mirror each other, and out of the play of reflections images arise, around which we may build our existence. Meeting and *choice* are hence the existential dimensions of the city. Through meeting and choice we gain a world, and remember Wittgenstein's words: "I am my world."[54] When we have a world, we dwell, in the sense of gaining an individual identity within a complex and often contradictory fellowship. Both aspects are important: fellowship means sharing in spite of diversity, identity means not to succumb to uniformity. The city, thus, ought to offer a sense of belonging in spite of individual choice. When this is the case, we possess a common place, and may say: "I am a New Yorker" or, "I am a Roman."

The question then arises: What is the meaning of such a self-identification? Or in other words: Which are the *contents* of the urban meeting? When Kahn says "a small boy may see something," he implies that a multitude of activities are presented to him, and that these activities reveal the world they belong to. We could also say that life is presented in its multifarious richness. But Kahn does not talk about life "as such." He says: "A city is a place where...," telling us that it is the *city* which makes the revelation of life possible. Life and place belong together, and the purpose of the city is that kind of revelation we have called meeting. Kahn's word "something" moreover suggests that life is structured. It always takes place "as something," and we always participate "as somebody," that is, on the basis of the choice of "something." Collective dwelling, thus, is not a mere coming together, but a being in the world somewhere as somebody. It is the somewhere, the place, which makes life visible. It fixes or keeps life, in the sense of a record or image which remains, explains and invites. Therefore we are conditioned by the place; we gain our identity when we choose among the images it offers, and may for instance say: "I am a Roman."

The term "somebody" implies a set of chosen activities. Thus we say: "I am a carpenter," "I am a merchant," or "I am an architect." The chosen activities make a certain mode of being in the world manifest; they are *hypotheses* of reality and as such based on three forms of understanding: practical, theoretical and poetical. The practical understanding of being in the world is the basis of what since Antiquity is known as the *vita activa*. Its manifestations are work (production) and politics, that is, the coordination of practical activities determined by certain ends. The theoretical understanding or *vita contemplativa* aims at revealing the order inherent in the world, be it "divine harmony" or "natural laws." It moreover serves to define the aims of practical life. Its manifestations are philosophy and science. The poetic understanding or *vita poetica* grasps the world as a given totality of interrelated things. That is, it reveals the "thingness of things" and thus explains what things in truth *are*. Its manifestation is the work of art, where the understood truth is "set into work."

As hypotheses of reality the manifestations of the three forms of understanding reveal a world. Evidently this world is general as well as circumstantial. A mere general understanding would remain outside life, whereas a circumstantial understanding would disappear without leaving any trace. Settlements, and in particular capital cities, therefore gather a world which is proximal as well as distant, and relates what comes from afar to what is close at hand. We have already discussed this problem in connection with the center, and now understand that a center is a place where what is known is gathered, to allow for a choice inspired by explanations of the things gathered. This "explanation" resides in the very fact of meeting. When activities and things are brought together, they explain each other reciprocally and enter into what we have called a mirror-play of meanings which are kept by works of architecture. Thus the city is a place where we may discover something, in the sense of distinguishing it from other things. As our choice forms part of a totality, however, it does not isolate us, but rather allows for participation. Again we recognize the profound meaning of using the place as our primary self-identification. It implies respect for the totality in which we take part, and the realization that our part is meaningful because it belongs to a world. Thus we say "I am a Roman" before we say "I am a carpenter."

Meeting and choice may also be related to the general functions of orientation and identification. Meeting, thus, is basically an act of orientation, whereas choice implies identification. When we

identify with a certain activity or role within a fellowship, we also indentify in a more general sense with the totality to which the role belongs. We cannot possibly identify with everything, as it is a basic human condition that an individual cannot "have everything." And still, one attains everything indirectly through participation. It goes without saying, however, that choice in many historical situations was limited by social class or hereditary patterns, and thus predetermined or imposed.

As a record of meeting the city is an artifact. It is made by man deliberately to allow for choice. The possibilities offered, however, are not "invented" at random. On the contrary they are interpretations of what is given: practical activities which serve to cultivate what is there and thus to gain an economic foothold, theoretical assumptions which serve to define a position in space and time, and artistic forms which bring the concrete being of the inhabited world close. Urban experience consists in a sense of this multifarious reality; it tells us that life has many layers of meaning, and that these meanings cannot be separated from the here and the now.

The question then arises: How should the form of the settlement be to allow for meeting and choice? Evidently meeting implies that things are close together, or, in spatial terms, it means *density*. A city where the parts are scattered around, is no city. Rather the city has to surround us, tightly and firmly. This means that the buildings which constitute the settlement have to form "interiors" which are perceived as such. The experience does not consist in an adding up of buildings, but in the spontaneous awareness of a superior form which is called *urban space*. When we describe an urban experience, we use prepositions such as "with-

in," "between," "under," "over," "in front of," "behind," "next to," etc., that is, relationships which indicate a varied but integrated spatial organization. In general, density is the complement to the figural quality we have recognized as the primary "exterior" property of the settlement.

Meeting, however, also implies *variety*. To point this out might seem trival, but the need for variety immediately poses the problem of *unity*. How do diverse elements form a totality, a place? Is it only a question of density, that is, of the Gestalt principle of proximity, or is there something else to it? Evidently the formation of urban spaces requires something more than simple togetherness.

The experience of a totality cannot be entirely *staccato*, but is basically a continuous process. In addition to density and variety we may therefore include *continuity* as a fundamental property of the urban interior. To allow for meeting and choice, these three qualities have to be present, and should reveal themselves when we enter the settlement. Thus we may say: "I am here," not in the sense of a final accomplished fact, but as the beginning of a life of discovery and choice. The three properties may of course be more or less strong; in local centers variety is for instance less important than in a capital city which gathers a more comprehensive world.

Density, variety and continuity are general properties. To understand urban form, they have to be related to the primary kinds of urban spaces, which, on the basis of what has been said on center and path in the first chapter, may be defined as *square* and *street*. Our discussion of the morphology and topology of urban space has to take these elements as its point of departure.

Morphology

It might seem strange to start a discussion on urban space with morphological rather than topological considerations. Urban spaces, however are, like any kind of place, conditioned by the built form of the boundaries. It is the built form which determines the *Stimmung* or local character, and it is the built form which makes continuity and variety manifest. At the outset, space is experienced as a general sense of being within, and only through closer acquaintance it develops into a coherent, structured image.[55] Built form, however, is immediately there, and if it possesses local characteristics, we may spontaneously say: "now I am in Paris," or, "now I am in Venice." This implies that the built form should not only give presence to those activities which are gathered by the place, but that the visualization should happen in a certain way, to constitute a particular "here." Continuity therefore means something more than linear succession; it also means that variety ought to appear as variations on conspicuous local "themes."

The urban *street* usually appears as a succession of such variations. The same unit is repeated, but never exactly alike. Thus the street becomes a manifestation of the process of discovery. We are led on step by step, being always "here," but at each step the here reveals another possibility of itself. The meeting which takes place in the street is a direct and immediate one; we are exposed to what is there, although we ourselves may remain anonymous. Variety therefore has to occur on the ground on which we stand and move, it has to be together with us. A few conclusions concerning the built form of the street may be derived from these considerations. General continuity has to be combined with relatively small, varied units at eye level, whereas the upper parts of the wall (facade) may show a more uniform movement. (If it is completely regular, however, the varieties below may seem caprices rather than variations on themes.) The upper conclusion or silhouette naturally does not play that primary role we discovered when discussing the exterior aspect of the settlement. The perception of a silhouette demands a certain distance (*Fernsicht*), whereas the street is always experienced from near at hand (*Nahsicht*).[56] And still, the silhouette contributes to the definition of the units which constitute the wall, and also to determine its character when rising towards the sky. What is here indicated, first of all holds true for public streets connected with production and distribution. Basically, however, streets where special activities take place or domestic streets need a similar continuous differentiation, albeit to a lesser degree.

Examples which illustrate the general qualities of the street are of course legion. This is already an interesting fact in itself, as it shows that the simple form of the urban wall is capable of innumerable variations, and thus of constituting ever new places. Its capacity is due to the possible use of a hierarchy of themes, with the built unit as a superior type allowing for varied repetition, whereas doors, windows and other elements act as subordinate themes. Even in large cities such as Paris and Amsterdam the form of the urban wall is based on a few themes which appear throughout. The character of the urban wall is also often determined by the way of making, in addition to the formal themes. Thus it may appear as being soft or hard, thick or thin, rough or smooth, or as a combination of such qualities. In Barcelo-

51. *Unity and variety: Innsbruck.*   52. *Urban ceiling: Florence.*

na, for instance, numerous buildings from different periods show a characteristic unified, block-like form with applied, intensely expressive details and a vibrating surface.

The wall is the primary boundary of urban space, because it records the contents of the meeting which here takes place. The floor does not have such a function; it rather serves as a "neutral" ground, which because of its general extension, plays a unifying and characterizing role. Since it should not make variety manifest, the urban floor ought to be distinguished by continuous patterns and by good maintenance.[57] A shabby and broken floor is usually more disturbing to the cityscape than derelict buildings! The floor pattern may of course be coordinated with the articulation of the urban wall, to give emphasis to movements and to distinguish zones. The urban "ceiling" is in general the sky, but its appearance is conditioned by the upper termination of the buildings. In the classical South the urban wall usually terminates with more or less continuous horizontals which make the sky appear as a distant and stable background. In the romantic North, however, the variable atmospheric conditions of the sky are caught by a complex silhouette. It ought to be repeated that the street is primarily distinguished by its horizontal rhythm which expresses the process of meeting and discovery. The vertical tensions only contribute to define the general atmosphere within which this process unfolds. Streets do not necessarily lead to a particular goal. The studies of Kevin Lynch show that they often start and end without precise definition and are characterized by what happens along them.[58] When they are goal-oriented, it means that the movement becomes a kind of preparation for a choice which is expressed by a point of

arrival, that is, by a square and usually by one or more dominant public buildings.

The intersection of streets, or crossing, is an urban space of particular interest. First, it implies a possible change of direction, that is, a more general kind of choice. Second, it slows down the continuous movement of the street. The crossing may hence be considered a "quasi-square"; it intensifies the sense of meeting, opens up new aspects of the place, and invites us to reflect on the contents of the environment. The crossing is therefore often emphasized by particular formal means, such as corner pilasters (e.g. the Addizione Erculea of Ferrara), fountains (e.g. the Quattro Fontane in Rome), or diagonally placed projections or towers (e.g. the Ensanche of Barcelona). Another interesting case of the meeting of urban spaces is the point where a street opens into a square (*Strasseneinmündung*).[59] Paul Zucker characterizes the *square* as a "psychological parking place within the civic landscape" and moreover says that it "makes the community a community and not merely an aggregate of individuals."[60] The term "parking place" suggests that the process of discovery here has come to a conclusion. Movement is stopped, and we find time to rest and meditate on the contents of the meeting. That is, the square does not necessarily make a particular choice manifest, often it rather condenses what is spread out along the street into one complex but comprehensive image. Choice is thus facilitated, at the same time as the world of the community as perceived as a whole. Sometimes, however, the square represents an agreement, and appears as an "explanation" of the multifarious world of its environment. In many medieval cities both kinds were present; the market, thus, took

care of the function of meeting, whereas the *parvis* prepared for the more articulate explanation of the cathedral.[61] In Rome, the two kinds are represented respectively by Piazza Navona and St. Peter's Square. In any case the square fulfills the gathering function of the settlement. It represents the meaning of coming together, a fact which is proved by the common root of the words "town" and "tun," the latter denoting the courtyard of a farm in the Scandinavian languages. Since the original meaning of "tun" is fence or boundary (German: *Zaun*), it also shows that urban space is determined by the enclosing built form.

It follows from the nature of the square that its boundary ought to offer a stronger sense of unity than the street, and at the same time a richer articulation. The wall themes which characterize the place are here presented in their most conspicuous form, and the variations have to be kept within reasonable limits. The rhythm becomes more regular, whereas the vertical tensions are emphasized. Horizontal movement slows down to become a kind of vibration within a general equilibrium, and surprises are left out. Rather than offering the experience of something new, the square therefore tells us how things *are*. Simultaneously the vertical tensions relate the phenomena of daily life down on the ground to the sky above, and explain life as a way of being in the "between." The square thus appears as a complementary form to the "exterior" of the settlement. The sense of arrival is here fulfilled; what was a promise when the settlement was seen from the outside, becomes an understood world. In the old cities of the Low Countries this relationship between exterior, street and square is particularly evident. When seen from afar, the gabled roofs appear over the

Røisheim i 1892

Wilse Enerett
1375 L

engirdling city wall and state the basic theme of the settlement. In the streets the theme becomes subject to innumerable variations, and when we finally arrive in the square, it is presented to us as it "is." We may compare with a musical composition where the fully developed theme only appears at the end, after having been prepared for a thorough series of suggestions.[62] The experience of explanation thereby offered, is enhanced when the theme is taken over by a public building which acts as a focus and common symbol. Such a building usually rises out of the mass of houses, and when seen from afar already offers a promise of the understood world hidden inside. The exterior and interior of old cities therefore complemented each other and constituted a meaningful whole. Man did not only visit the city to discover possibilities, but to come to an understanding of these as parts of an integrated (albeit complex) world. Thus his personal choice gained the meaning of a case of collective dwelling.

What has been said above about the floor and the ceiling of the street, in general also pertains to the square. The floor, thus, acts as a continuous, integrating ground, a function which may be emphasized by a regular, geometrical pattern. Sometimes the pattern may focus attention on a public building of particular importance, as is the case at the Campo in Siena. Interruptions in the surface may damage or enhance the sense of unity of the place, and should therefore be based on careful considerations of the totality. The "ceiling" is a function of the upper termination of the surrounding buildings, which here gain an increased importance due to the larger dimensions of the space. The particular kind of standing and rising which distinguishes the buildings of a settlement, is therefore

revealed more clearly around the square than elsewhere. Together, wall, floor and ceiling define the character of urban space and invite man to identify and dwell.

The morphology of traditional urban spaces was studied in an imaginative way at the beginning of our century by Raymond Unwin and Albert Erich Brinckmann,[63] and has been revived recently by Rob Krier.[64] So far, however, the problem has been presented in purely formalistic terms. When we interpret urban space as a function of meeting and choice, the formal considerations are given an existential basis, and may be understood as manifestation of collective dwelling. Thus we will no longer be afraid of talking about how the things which surround us "look," and gain a new contact with what is there. To identify with a place primarily means to be open to its character or *genius loci*, and to have a place in common means to share the experience of the local character. To respect the place, finally, means to adapt new buildings to this character. Identification and adaptation evidently presuppose an understanding of the built form which embodies the *genius loci*. We shall later consider this problem in more detail in connection with the discussion of public buildings and houses.

Topology

We have called the kind of space which satisfies the demand for density, urban space, and have singled out the street and the square as its primary manifestations. Urban spaces have to possess particular properties. First they have to be *enclosed*, in the sense of being "interiors." We could in this context transfer the concept of "figural quality" to space, and talk about "spatial figures." A spatial figure is a form

which is easily recognizable and possesses a conspicuous identity.

Evidently figural quality depends on the form as such, and on the size of the unit. A space which is very large will loose its identity, even if it has precisely defined boundaries. Figural quality therefore always relates to man; it is a function of life taking place rather than an abstract formal property. The problem of size has usually been understood as a question of "human scale," which does not necessarily mean dimensions which relate to man's body as such, but to the actions in which it takes part. In general, human scale is a function of meeting, that is, of coming together rather than being dispersed. The spatial form ought to facilitate this coming together. A street, thus, should be relatively narrow and have a defined direction, whereas a square as a matter of principle ought to be round (!). We have already pointed out the importance of continuous boundaries; freestanding buildings do not constitute urban space, especially if the distance between them is large. The figural quality of a street or square may thus be destroyed by the demolition of a single building.

To allow for meeting, urban spaces ought to be topological. Topological forms leave the constituent elements "free," as they do not impose any superior order. Hence we find that theorists who subscribe to Aristoteles' aim that the city should offer man security and *happiness*, tend to propose topologically organized urban space.[65]

In general, topological spaces do not possess any kind of defined symmetry, but are clearly enclosed. Geometrical spaces, on the contrary, represent a common order, and therefore suggest or impose certain choices. We have already pointed out that a comprehen-

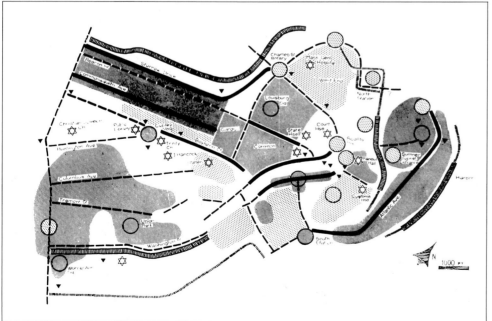

sive geometrical layout makes the settlement become an *imago mundi*. A straight and regular street, however, does not alone represent such a general symbolism; rather it visualizes a social agreement which also comprises a certain mode of being between earth and sky. Due to the importance of the square as a center, it acquires the quality of a comprehensive symbol when it is geometrized.[66] St. Peter's Square in Rome is undoubtedly an image of the world interpreted in Christian terms, and the Capitoline Hill an image of the center of the earth in its relation to the departures and returns of human life. The square, thus, condenses and visualizes the content which is less clearly expressed by the settlement as a whole. Since this content primarily consists in human meeting, the square ought to possess topological characteristics in addition to its geometrical aspects. The Campo in Siena is a fine example of such a meaningful equilibrium between freedom and order, as is St. Mark's Square in Venice. In a large city like Rome, the functions of the square are specialized, with Piazza Navona acting as a comprehensive *microcosmos.*

We have already pointed out the affinity between meeting and orientation, and ought to add a few words about the relationship between orientation and urban space. Thanks to the pioneering research of Kevin Lynch, the problem is well understood.[67] First of all, Lynch tells us that the primary objects of orientation are street and square (often in connection with conspicuous "landmarks"). Thus he departs from the abstract interpretation of space characteristic of modern architecture, and returns to a concrete approach in terms of spatial figures. He moreover shows that we orientate relative to the "districts" or "domains" which are

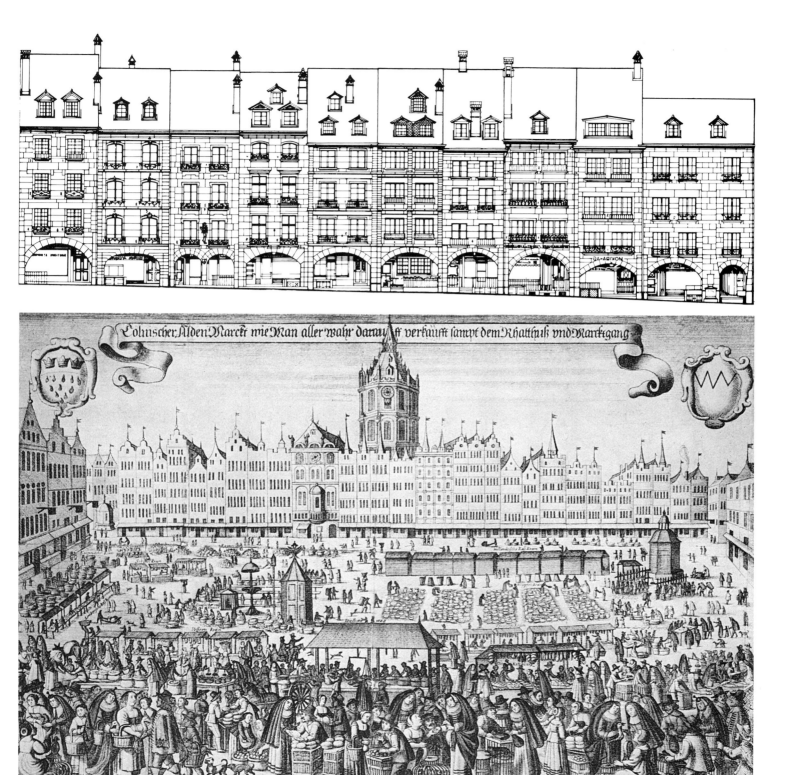

delimited by the network of streets and squares. Evidently, the three spatial elements correspond to the categories of cluster, row and enclosure, which pertain to the settlement as a whole and furthermore to the Gestalt principles of organization. The domain, thus, is in principle a cluster, the street a row, and the square an enclosure. Urban space therefore repeats on a smaller scale the more comprehensive orders; it condenses the world and thereby brings it close. We could also consider this relationship between the environmental levels the other way around, pointing out that the cluster, row and enclosure are determined from within, with the urban spaces acting as generating cells. In villages the two levels may coincide completely, and we understand how the spatial figures of settling and meeting are basically the same. In both cases the figures admit patterns of togetherness and make collective dwelling manifest. Through orientation we attain a spatial image of the place. This image defines our possibility of movement, and hence of discovery and choice. If we do not possess an environmental image, we just ramble about without any sense of belonging. In smaller towns the formation of a comprehensive image is fairly easy, whereas larger cities favor partial images in terms of known neighborhoods and particularly prominent spaces. To facilitate the latter kind of image-making, cities ought to be subdivided into districts defined by "edges" such as streets, shores and embankments. It goes without saying that a spatial image may be topological, geometrical, or a combination of both. The presence of topological properties, that is, proximity, continuity and enclosure, is a presupposition for the formation of a satisfactory image, whereas more regular geometrical

spaces usually act as focal points within the extended topological fabric. Paradoxically, a completely regular geometrical layout may impede orientation due to the similarity of its parts, although it may easily be grasped mentally. The sense of disorientation is particularly strong when a clearly defined hierarchy of primary and subordinate spaces is lacking. We understand, thus, that environmental image and spatial organization do not necessarily coincide. The image is a function of "lived space," whereas organization often becomes an abstract pattern which is only recognizable from the air.[68] We may conclude that a city ought to comprise topological as well as geometrical elements in terms of a hierarchy of urban spaces in order to allow for life taking place.

Typology
Together the built form and the spatial layout of streets and squares constitute those *urban figures* which make collective dwelling manifest. A settlement is mainly remembered because of its urban figures (as well as its landmarks), and in the old city atlases important cities are often represented by *vedute* of their principal squares.[69] The city so to speak consists of its urban spaces, and to know these means to be familiar with the place as a whole. The intervening "domains" usually remain more or less unknown and only partake in the environmental image as generalized textures.
Figural quality implies a form which is of general value, that is, something typical and common. Strange inventions are not true figures, since figural quality depends on recognition. Thus the figure transcends the individual situation and becomes the symbol of a world. It would, however, be a misunderstanding to put a sign of equation

between figure and type. The type is the general point of departure common to many worlds, whereas the figure represents its setting into work in the here and now.
The question then arises whether it is possible to establish a typology of urban spaces. A classification may be based on functional or formal aspects, or a combination of both. Thus we may talk about "domestic," "mercantile" or "monumental" spaces, and imply certain differences in topological-geometrical layout. But such a survey would only bring us one step towards an understanding of the typology which determines the urban figure. A figure is recognized as such because it possesses pronounced qualities; it is a *strong Gestalt*, in a very concrete sense. Architectural history in fact knows such spaces. The colonnaded or arcaded street is a good example. The main thoroughfare of the ancient Roman cities were distinguished by rows of columns on both sides, and were thus endowed with a meaning which transcends the content of the *botteghe* behind.[70]
Not only do the columns indicate a superior order, but they also "populate" the street with "typical" anthropomorphic elements. The arcaded street has a long tradition in many countries, and usually makes a kind of varied order manifest. The main street of Bern, the *Gerechtigkeitsgasse-Kramgasse*, offers a particularly splendid example. Here the continuous arcades are varied throughout, as are the houses above, but the underlying typology is evident, and makes the urban space appear as a magnificent, unified figure. Other typical streets possessing a conspicuous identity, may be the result of the varied repetition of motifs such as bay-windows. In both examples the figural quality is connected with a cer-

63. Place Vendôme, Paris
(J.H. Mansart, 1698).

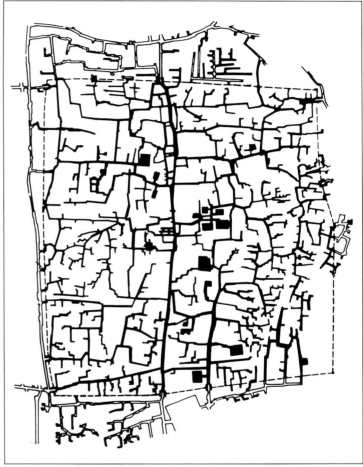

64. The Islamic city, Cairo.

tain interpretation of the relationship between the urban space and the interiors of the adjacent buildings. This is a most significant fact, since the meeting which is visualized by the street obviously implies a particular kind of interaction between outside and inside. Thus the wall becomes the expression of a "meeting of interior and exterior forces of use and space," to quote the words of Robert Venturi.[71]

The history of the square also comprises a series of typical figures. As examples we may single out the Roman *forum* with its axial layout and the French *Place Royale* of the seventeenth century with its centrally located statue of the sovereign. Paul Zucker calls the two types "directed" and "nuclear" squares,[72] and thus points out how a spatial figure needs a system of centers and axes to become something more than a mere enclosure. Evidently the use of centers (defined by monuments or fountains) and directions do not imply strict symmetry, as is proved by the "dynamic equilibrium" of the Piazza della Signoria in Florence.[73]

Regular symmetry may on the contrary kill the gathering quality of the square, as is proved by numerous examples from the eighteenth and nineteenth centuries.

It is beyond the scope of this book to enter into a detailed discussion of historical and possible typologies. Let us only add that the choice of urban figures expresses a mode of being in the world, that is, on earth under the sky. A comparison of European and Islamic cities illustrates that. Whereas the former give primary importance to a system of streets and squares which bring an inhabited landscape consisting of natural places close to man, the Islamic city represents in principle an answer to the problem of dwelling in the *desert*, that is, in a place-less landscape of infinite, monotonous expanse. The settlement pattern which better answers the challenge of the desert is the dense, topological labyrinth. Islamic cities, thus, are constituted through an addition of enclosed court-houses, and the urban spaces become leftover intervals, seemingly irregular, but in reality organized according to the patterns of Islamic society. The characteristic blind alley, thus, makes the family unit environmentally manifest.[74] The main spatial dimension of the desert is the *horizontal*, and the Arabs have in fact preferred low, horizontally extended buildings. The only vertical element is the slender needle of the minaret, which reminds man that he also lives under the sky. In the desert man does not encounter the multifarious "forces" of nature, but experiences its most general, "cosmic" properties. The mosque is therefore organized over a regular, orthogonal pattern, and brings an element of general order into the labyrinthine settlement.

In general, urban spaces keep and visualize the world of collective dwelling. Three functions may here be distinguished. First, urban spaces allow collective life to take place, admitting all the various activities of a society. The spaces, however, are also related to the topographical structure of the natural environment. Second, the built form in its standing and rising expresses a common mode of being between earth and sky, which constitutes the primary identity of the collectivity. Third, the spatial figures which serve as organizing foci within the urban texture, may visualize a more comprehensive understanding of the world. The last function may gain such a profound general value that the space appears as a center to the whole world, as is the case on the Capitoline Hill in Rome.

Urban space today

The actual loss of place mentioned in connection with the settlement as a whole, corresponds to a loss of urban space. The spatial continuum of the "green" city did not allow for traditional streets and squares, and theorists of modern planning in fact advocated their total abolition.[75] As a result, the cities of today tend to become a mere agglomeration of separate buildings. Even the old cities have become subject to a process of disintegration, partly because of a general dispersion of functions and partly because of the pressure of mechanized traffic. The possibility of meeting and choice is thereby lost, and human alienation becomes a normal state of affairs. One of the persons interviewed by Kevin Lynch during his study of Los Angeles expressed it with these words: "It's as if you were going somewhere for a long time, and when you got there you discovered there was nothing there, after all."[76]

The present reaction against the green city, however, has brought about a renewed sense of urban space. Although modern society at the moment does not know the function of meeting in the traditional sense, many start to realize that a city without defined spaces does not offer any kind of promise. Many theorists and practising architects therefore carry through studies of historical cities, to recall the principles of urban morphology and topology. The general aim is to recover the city as a work of art, as is proposed in Aldo Rossi's book *The Architecture of the City*.[77] As a work of architecture, the city ought to visualize a world, and thus to allow for collective dwelling. Without an existentially founded theory of the urban functions, however, the "architecture of the city" easily becomes an empty form. This

danger is in fact proved by numerous actual projects, where the spatial figures of the past are copied without understanding their nature as "gatherings" and "explanations." This is especially the case in projects where geometrical patterns which remind of the exercises at the academies of the nineteenth century, are mistaken for true figural quality. In spite of these unfortunate tendencies, however, many important symptoms indicate that we are on the way towards a recovery of authentic urban spaces.

To conclude, we may again remind of the basic importance of the *genius loci*. Even in our "global" epoch, the spirit of place remains a reality. Human identity presupposes the identity of place, and the *genius loci* therefore ought to be understood and preserved. Urban space visualizes a world which is general as well as local, and thereby helps the buildings which serve public and private dwelling to be rooted in the given environment. We could also say that it prepares for the fulfillment of dwelling in the institution and the house.

IV. Institution

Within the settlement we find buildings which make the common values of the inhabitants manifest. Choices have been made, and on the basis of *agreement*, dwelling has become public. We could also say that dwelling has been structured as a set of *institutions*, which explain the world. "I am" no longer is an open mirror, but now consists in the identification with particular meanings. Thus we may accept a hypothesis about the general nature of the world, an understanding of a given locality, or a theory about how society ought to be organized. In the settlement these agreements ought to be fixed and visualized by public buildings. Evidently these buildings allow the actions of common consent to take place, but moreover they have to give concrete presence to the meaning of these actions as a way of life or a mode of being-in-the-world.

When we stand in front of a public building, it should offer the promise of an explanation of how things are by gathering and ordering the multifarious meeting of the *urbs* into a synthetic image or figure. And when we enter, the promise ought to be fulfilled by a space which appears as a meaningful *microcosmos*. The public building, thus, is an *imago mundi*, but always "as something," as "church," as "city hall," as "theater," as "museum," as "school." In other words, the public building is not an abstract symbol, but partakes in daily life, which it relates to what is timeless and common. In the church a general understanding of world and life is made present, in the city hall the organization of society, in the theater life as it is lived, in the museum the memories of mankind, and in the school our experience as knowledge and advice. When we "use" these institutions the world is opened up, and belonging is realized.

Public dwelling, however, does not imply uniformation. When we face and enter the public building, we always bring with us our personal "somebody" as a contribution to the agreement. In the theater and the school our individual identities are part of the very function, whereas in the church and city hall they are rather taken into consideration through ritual and ceremony. When the Gothic cathedral is called a "mirror of the world," one does not only refer to its cosmic and religious symbolism, but also to its comprehensive presentation of the daily life of man.[78] A public building would in fact remain an abstract generalization, if it did not in this way incorporate the here and now.

The public building therefore relates to the *vita activa* as well as the *vita contemplativa*; it is an integral image, and as such both a goal and a point of departure. Here man finds that insight he needs to be able to carry out his actions with a sense of purpose and meaning. As a work of architecture, the building is the result of a poetic understanding of the world. Only the *vita poetica* makes it possible for man to translate his practical and theoretical understanding into a concrete image, and to perceive its meaning. Public dwelling, therefore, does not only consist in social identification, but in a poetical relationship to the shared world.

We have already defined the shared world as a gathering of things and a meeting of human beings, some coming from afar and some being already here. We have also pointed out that this gathering is as a rule related to a given natural environment, which through the very process of gathering, becomes an "inhabited landscape." The public building, therefore, is not only "something," but also "somewhere"; a church is for instance different here and there, although it always remains the "same." The concept of "center" therefore has a double meaning. The settlement is a center to the landscape, as it brings the landscape close to man. The public building is a center in a deeper sense, as it *explains* the landscape and thus relates it to the world in general. The choices that are demanded by the the the urban spaces, are accordingly inspired by the institutions, which serve as illuminating centers of meaning. Here what remains hidden in the city is revealed, and life is freed from its seeming arbitrariness. When this happens, we dwell in the sense of sharing and participation.

What, then, are the means which make public dwelling manifest? To answer the question, we have to return to our concepts of embodiment and admittance. The built form embodies the way something is between earth and sky, whereas organized space admits its actions. In both cases a relationship between outside and inside comes into play, where the exterior acts as a preparation for the interior. The built form is facade as well as interior elevation, and spatial organization consists in a path which leads from the outside towards a goal within. Distinct and meaningful figures are thus created, which serve as objects of human identification. As synthetic explanations, these figures ought to possess a high degree of formal precision, at the same time as they comprise the complexities of the gathered world. The public figure therefore stands forth as simultaneously simple and rich; it is easily imageable but invites for contemplation of its comprehensive content. Variety here becomes articulate form and density ordered composition. Does the public image ignore the contradictions inherent in any fellowship? Not at all. It is a basic quality of the artistic form that it may embody contents which are logically contradictory. A work of art is always a case of "both-and," to use again the words of Robert Venturi.[79] The artistic explanation in fact consists in revealing meanings that are not accessible to logical analyses. Architectural history, however, shows that contradictions may be more or less pronounced. During the Quattrocento they were generally minimized in favor of the ideal of an all-comprehending "harmony," whereas the Cinquecento as a reaction against this simplification excelled in complex and contradictory solutions. The works of the Cinquecento were *solutions*, however, both in the sense of meaningful syntheses and powerful figures. Michelangelo's architecture proves that.[80]

The following discussion of the morphology and topology of the public building cannot possibly cover all its manifestations. Rather we shall use one major example to illuminate the problems. Throughout the course of Western history, the *church* was a leading building task.[81] In the church man's understanding of the cosmos, as well as his own life in the world was kept and visualized. Over and over again new interpretations of something general and timeless were offered, and over and over again the church served to give man the sense of an existential foothold. Thus the church illustrates what architecture is all about, and teaches us how to use its "language."

Morphology

We have already explained how a built form embodies a way of being in the world through its standing, rising and opening. We have also pointed out that the embodiment always happens "as something." Even if a city hall and a

church belong to the same community, they will make its basic meanings manifest in a different way. This is evident in many medieval cities where church and city hall are neighbors. We could also say that the worlds gathered by the two buildings only in part overlap; in the city hall the earthly aspects are emphasized, whereas the church gives pride of place to more general, "heavenly" meanings. The diversity is often expressed by a different treatment of the towers which signal the presence of the two institutions within the settlement. Since the church offers a more comprehensive explanation, it has, together with its predecessor, the temple, in general been the main generator of those forms which characterize the habitat. Throughout European history, thus, the embodiment of meanings has been determined from "above."[82] The explanation offered by the church radiated out to the environment, and made the other institutions as well as the houses appear as reflections of the truth it embodied.

At the outset, the church was primarily an interior form. The exterior of the Early Christian basilica, thus, was conceived as a neutral "envelope" around the articulate, symbolic interior. This fact already tells us something important about the world which is here made manifest. In contrast to the Greek temple, the church does not take the natural characters as its point of departure, translating them into bodily forms which reveal the understood landscape,[83] but aims at a more general interpretation of the relationship between earth and sky. The origins of this interpretation are the first words of the first chapter of the Genesis: "In the beginning God created the heavens and the earth." That is, in the beginning a *place* was given to

make creation possible. Everything that comes into being is between earth and sky, and in general represents a conquest of *chaos*. "The earth was formless and empty, darkness was over the surface of the deep..." Creation, thus, is opposed to certain "properties" of chaos: emptiness, formlessness, darkness and fathomless depth. How, then, is chaos conquered? Emptiness and formlessness can only be won by substance and order, darkness by light, and depth by a solid ground. Hence light appears, as well as the order of up and down, and the dry land. A *spatiality* is here indicated, which is the presupposition for life. This spatiality is intended in *concrete*, rather than abstract-mathematical, terms. The space of creation is not empty and infinite, but determined by "things." Thus it is a place. Now life may "take place," as "plants and trees bearing seed according to their kinds," and as "living creatures according to their kinds."

In the second chapter of the Genesis the togetherness of place and creatures is described as a garden. Then "the Lord God took the man and put him in the Garden of Eden to work it and to take care of it." Human life in the Christian interpretation is therefore from the beginning seen in relation to place, and the primary task of man is defined as work and care. We could also say that man's care is expressed in his works.

Man's works are multifarious, and among them we find the work of architecture, the building.[84] When man "builds" the world, he visualizes the spatiality of creation, both in the sense of a general relationship between earth and sky, and in the sense of a particular "here." This spatiality is always related to man through care and work, and therefore becomes manifest "as something"; as house, as school, as church. Buildings are also between earth and sky "according to their kinds." How a building stands, rises and opens expresses its kind. In "standing there," the building admits life to take place and at the same time it embodies the life-situation as an intelligible character. Thus the building attains figural quality.

As a place, the church embodies the basic properties of the world of creation. All other buildings make partial worlds manifest; the church aims at generality. This means that it should make the relationship between earth and sky visible as it is. Which, then, are the constant and which are the temporal aspects of this relationship? The earth always remains the dark, bearing ground of rocks, water and vegetation, and the sky the domain of light, atmosphere and the cardinal points. The earth, thus, is substance and form, the sky illumination and order. And their relationship is always the difference between down and up, that is, between horizontal and vertical. Temporal, however, are the choices between the properties of earth and sky, as well as the interpretation of their meeting. The inner elevation of the church has always made these contents visible. In the Early Christian basilica, thus, we find two superimposed zones: below, the colonnade or arcade accompanied by a dark aisle, and above, the high wall or clerestory pierced by large windows and covered by glittering mosaics. Remembering the natural and anthropomorphic symbolism of the column and the heavenly symbolism of light, we understand how this elevation embodies basic meanings of earth and sky.

Through the following centuries the theme became subject to ever new interpretations, from the increasingly strong integration of the two zones in Romanesque and Gothic architecture, to the geometric coordination during the Renaissance, and the illusionary interplay of the Baroque *teatrum sacrum*. Thousands of churches were built, and the basic theme always remained the same. And still, hardly two of these churches were alike, just as men are different although they all stand up in space. To be able to read and interpret the inner elevation of the church, one has to understand it as a composite image which comprises subordinate images such as the column, the arch and the window. All of these elements gather aspects of the world, and together they make existential spatiality manifest.[85]

In our brief discussion of the elevation of ecclesiastical space, we have only considered its vertical organization. The horizontal rhythm, however, may also serve to explain basic properties of the world. A particularly interesting example is offered by Alberti's Sant'Andrea in Mantua.[86] In place of aisles the nave is here accompanied by an alternation of open and closed chapels which form a rhythmical succession of wide and narrow intervals, between pilasters. The rhythm is carried on but varied in transept and chancel. Following the musical theory of the epoch, the widths of the intervals are proportioned according to the ratios of the consonances. In the nave, thus, the ratio is 1:2, in the transept 2:3, and in the apse, finally, it has become a perfect 1:1. Evidently Alberti wanted to show how the harmony increases as we approach the altar, which represents the meaningful core of the built "explanation."

Sant'Andrea may also serve as a point of departure for a brief discussion of the built form of the exterior, that is, the facade. Here the "wall theme" of

72. *The integration of heaven and earth: King's College Chapel, Cambridge (1446 ff.).*

73. *The teatrum sacrum of the Baroque: Vierzehnheiligen (B. Neumann 1743 ff.).*

74. *S. Andrea, Mantua (L.B. Alberti, 1470 ff.).*

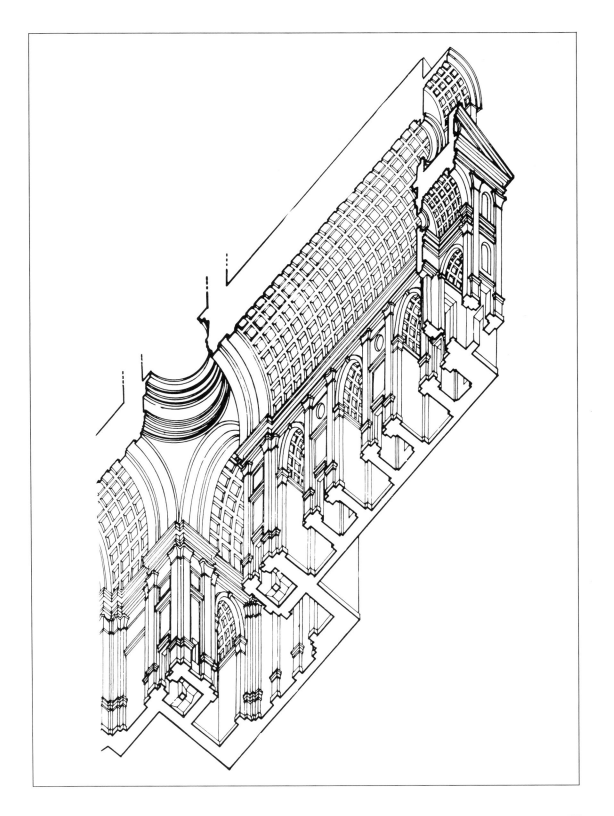

the interior also appears, but this time the central interval is considerably wider than those on the sides; the ratio is in fact 1:3. Two aims are here satisfied: first, the creation of an inviting entrance, and, second, an adaptation to the complex, dissimilar forms of the surroundings. We understand, thus, that the facade was intended as a transitory figure which interrelates the exterior and the interior. A certain analogy to the interior elevation thereby becomes apparent: the elevation acts as a transitory figure between earth and sky, whereas the facade mediates between outside and inside. In doing that, however, it prepares for the revelation of heaven in the interior. Thus it becomes a *porta coeli.*

The history of the church facade illustrates this meaning. In the Early Christian basilica the entrance was small and modest, expressing a contrast between the profane outside and the sacred inside. In the medieval cathedral it becomes grand and "transparent," making the presence of the church in the world manifest.[87] The Renaissance, on the contrary, does not open up, but treats the facade as a surface where the general cosmic order which is common to the outside and the inside is projected. The Baroque facade, finally, gives emphasis to the function of "invitation," with the aim of persuading people to enter and participate. The means used to set these different interpretations into work are perforation (movement in depth), horizontal rhythm (such as the Baroque emphasis on the central interval), and vertical tension (to prepare for the embodied explanation of the interior.)

What has been said about the interior elevation and the facade of the church in principle applies to any public building, although the concrete manifesta-

76. *Central and longitudinal space: Holy Sepulchre, Jerusalem (335 ff.).*

77. *The synthesis of central and longitudinal space: Hagia Sofia, Constantinople (537).*

78. *The combination of central and longitudinal space: S. Spirito, Florence (F. Brunelleschi, 1436 ff.) and Cathedral, Pavia (Bramante, 1488).*

tion varies according to what the building "wants to be." Thus the facade is always a transitory element, and as such it has to possess a conspicuous figural quality which suggests a mode of being between earth and sky. Only thus it may stand forth in the urban environment and act as a goal. The interior is always explanation, and as such its built form has to reveal what is suggested inside. Hence it may satisfy our expectations and offer a sense of shared dwelling.

Topology

In the city many possible paths are given, and many goals are hidden. Thus we have to choose the direction of our movement and hope that it will lead somewhere. This "somewhere" is the public building, where obscurity and complexity become clarity and order. In other words, here path and goal are defined in terms of a systematically organized space. And, in fact, architectural history shows that public buildings generally are based on fundamental modes of organization, such as centralization, axiality and gridiron planning. The modes are used and combined differently according to the nature of the building task, and the degree of geometrization might vary. But the common denominator is the aim of giving man the sense of arrival in a place where a world is explained. We may again single out the church as a particularly illuminating example. As a building which should explain the most basic and general properties of the world, the church ought to reveal the essential nature of path and goal, both in relation to nature and to human life. The center of the Christian world, however, is something more than a concrete place of action. It is first of all the point where the meaning of life is revealed. This revelation presupposes

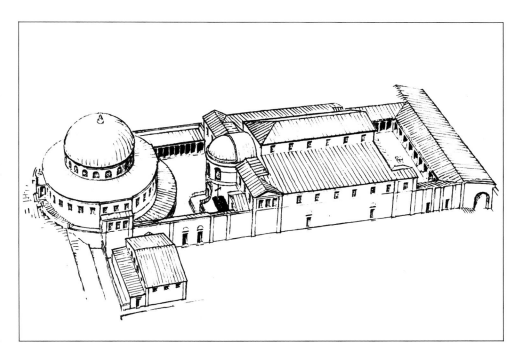

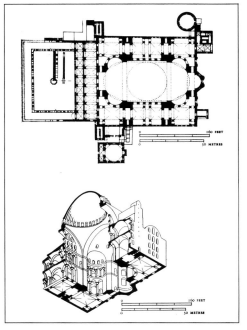

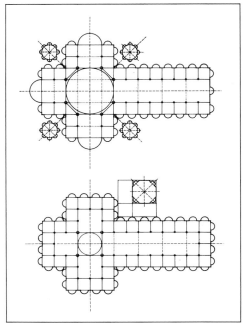

79. *Integration of central and longitudinal space by means of the oval: S. Carlo alle Quattro Fontane, Rome (F. Borromini, 1634 ff.).*

80. *"Pulsating" space: project for S. Filippo di Casale by G. Guarini (1671).*

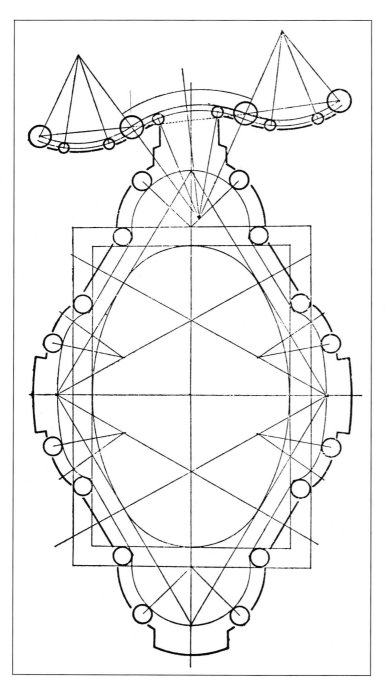

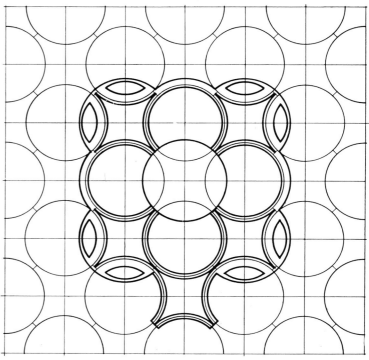

the following of Christ, which, in architectural terms, becomes manifest as a longitudinal axis leading to the altar, the symbol of the communion with Christ. When man returns to the world from this communion, he is ready to contribute to its transformation into a *Civitas Dei*.

From the beginning Christian architecture was international. The house of God does not belong to any particular place. God is where his plan of salvation is made visible. The same spatial theme is therefore found everywhere, representing a general Christian image of the spatiality of the world. It was introduced in the first major basilica built after Constantine's decree of 313, St. John in the Lateran in Rome, originally dedicated to Christus Salvator. The plan may be compared with the colonnaded street leading to the imperial throne in the Roman *palatium sacrum*.[88] Like the emperor, Christ was revealed at the end of a symbolic, axial succession of spaces. But early Christian architecture also developed another spatial theme: the static, centralized rotunda, which does not contain any pronounced direction. The latter solution was used for baptistries and mausoleums, that is, buildings which relate to what comes before and after man's life in the world. It is therefore deeply meaningful that the Church of the Holy Sepulchre in Jerusalem (ca. 335) consisted of a longitudinal basilica directed towards the site of the calvary, as well as a large rotunda, the *Anastasis*, over the tomb of Christ.

The history of ecclesiastical architecture shows ever new interpretations of the themes of axiality and centralization, as well as their combination. In the Eastern Empire, the centralized plan was adopted for the major churches, and in the Hagia Sophia in·Constantinople (537 ff.) a synthesis of centralization and longitudinality was achieved by adding half-domes on one of the axes of an immense, centrally placed baldachin. Thus the themes of path of salvation and Christ at the center were unified. During the following centuries such a combination appeared over and over again; in the West main emphasis was given to the longitudinal axis, whereas the East developed the Christocentric church. We may in this connection remind of the Latin cross of the Gothic cathedral and the Greek cross plans of Byzantine architecture. In some churches of the Renaissance a combination of the two themes was again attempted, culminating with the final scheme of St. Peter's in Rome. The Baroque aimed at full integration of path and center, and adopted the *oval* to solve the problem. Borromini's San Carlo alle Quattro Fontane, thus, is simultaneously longitudinal and centralized, and unites the basic properties of existential space to form one synthetic image. Guarini later developed this idea into "infinite" spatial fields where centers and axes become parts of "pulsating" organisms, which, according to Guarini himself, represent that "spontaneous action of dilation and contraction which is present throughout the whole living being."[89] Following Guarini, the protagonists of Late Baroque architecture in Central Europe conceived space as a combinatory system of interdependent "cells," which makes a multitude of configurations possible within the same comprehensive *continuum*. It is as if invisible existential space reveals itself and crystallizes in the building.[90] At the same time a complementary relationship between outside and inside is created. The explanation offered by the building therefore no longer appears as a "surprise," but rather as a result of the "living being" of existential space itself. Guarini interpreted this process in Christian terms, saying: "Divine Providence is the force that constitutes and informs the fragments of the world from within."[91]

The history of ecclesiastical architecture illustrates the principles of spatial composition, and shows how they can be set into work as volumetric figures which reveal existential spatiality. In Europe these figures were subject to historical change, although basic properties remained constant. Other cultures chose different figural possibilities in accordance with their interpretation of the world. The grid pattern of the Umayyad mosques, for instance, represents a visualization of the infinite "cosmic" space of the desert. Common to all cultures, however, are the general properties of concrete space and the demand for a precise spatial organization which serves to make the explanatory function of the public building manifest.

How, then, do these principles relate to modern architecture with its insistence on "free plan" and "spatial flow"? Although the free plan shunned axial and central symmetry, it is still based on directions and centers. Being developed in connection with the one-family house, it did not straight away apply to the public building.[92] Here a stronger sense of order seemed necessary to the pioneers, as is proved by Frank Lloyd Wright's early public structures: the Larkin Building (1904) and the Unity Church (1906). In the former axiality reappears and in the latter centralization, even at a time when Wright's general aim was the total "destruction of the box." During the later development of modern architecture, Mies van der Rohe reintroduced symmetrical layouts, and even in the topological plans of Aalto

81. *Umayyad mosque in Cairo.*

82. *Unity Church, Oak Park, Chicago (F.L. Wright, 1906).*

83. *National Gallery, Berlin (Mies van der Rohe, 1962).*

and Scharoun directions and centers are used to obtain spatial definition and figural quality. In Scharoun's Philharmonie, thus, the completely "free" plan of the engirdling lobby forms a zone of transition between the busy, urban world outside and the simultaneously centralized and axial order of the concert hall itself. After seeing the Philharmonie, the Dutch architect and planner Bakema remarked: "That is how we ought to build our cities."[93] It is tempting to infer that he recognized the meaningful relationship between the open topology of the surrounding spaces, and the symbolic order of the inner, "public" core, where music is placed at the center, as a force that illuminates "the fragments of the world from within."

Typology

The public building stands forth as a conspicuous figure which gathers and explains the environment. In his book on the construction of churches, Rudolf Schwarz talks about "the powerful figures which build the world."[94] We have demonstrated that these figures comprise built form and spatial organization, and visualize the basic relationship between earth and sky as well as the general structure of existential space. Therefore the church could act as a total *imago mundi*, bringing an inhabited world close to man. That the role of the public building was understood in the past, is proved by many old representations of cities, where nothing but the engirdling city wall and the landmarks within are shown.[95] The public buildings thus "constitute and inform" the city; they stand forth as figures which reveal reality. Our discussion of their morphology and topology has shown that certain properties of form and space are necessary to secure this role. It re-

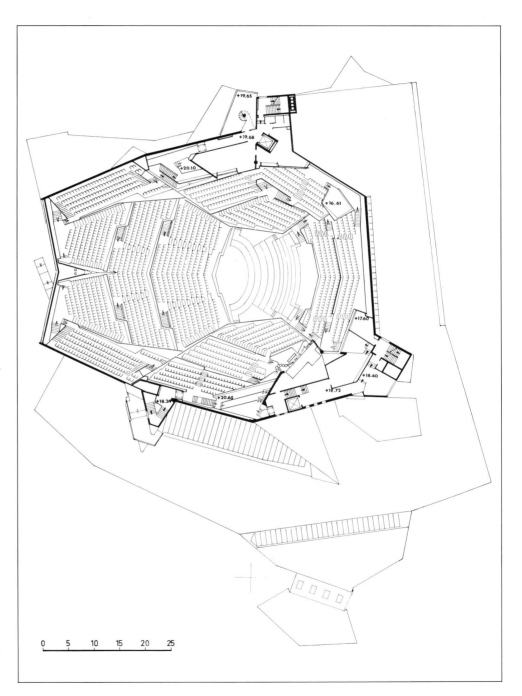

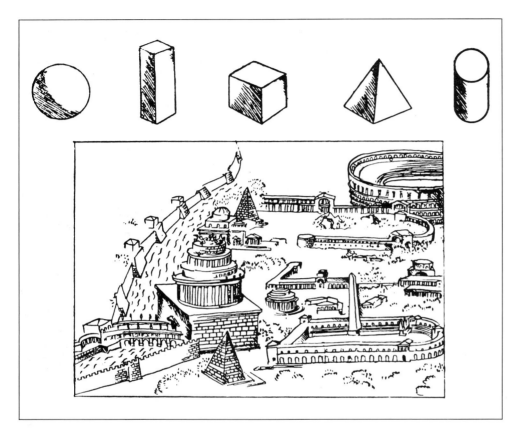

mains to say a few words about the figural quality of the public building in general.

We have already mentioned some of the most characteristic types, such as the basilica and the rotunda. Both are double functioning forms, in the sense of possessing figural quality both in their exterior and interior aspects. In general, their quality resides in the hierarchical symmetry of the volumetric composition, whereas the monotonous repetition of the hypostyle hall does not produce a similarly powerful image. Figural quality is therefore not the same as order; it rather presupposes a certain articulation which relates to man's life on earth under the sky. The basilica possesses this articulation in its concrete distinction between down and up, while the hypostyle hall places man within an abstract network of directions. Articulation as such, however, is not sufficient, as is proved by the caprices of innumerable late-modern buildings. A powerful, easily imageable overall form is imperative, and the basilica and the rotunda in fact possess this quality. Le Corbusier was therefore almost right when he defined architecture as "the masterly, correct and magnificent play of volumes brought together in light."[96]

He was *almost* right, because he understood volume in terms of "cubes, cones, spheres, cylinders and pyramids," that is, abstract geometrical forms, rather than concrete figures which stand on the ground and rise towards the sky.[97]

It might be added that the figural quality of a basilica or rotunda may be enhanced by the addition of other powerful images, such as the pediment and the dome. The former is a synthetic abbreviation of the tension between horizontal and vertical (as in any

86. The baldachin of St. Peter's
(Bernini, 1624).

kind of gable), whereas the latter also includes a reference to the horizon, and thus constitutes an integral *imago mundi*. Because of their easily imageable form and profound content, pediment and dome have for centuries served as primary distinguishing figures within the human habitat. As history shows, they may be subject to innumerable variations without losing their basic meaning. Because of its double exterior-interior function, the dome has been of particular importance, and towards the end of the nineteenth century it became usual to mark any public building with a dome. Originally, however, pediment and dome were considered *sacred* forms, and their use in secular buildings has at several occasions been met with criticism.[98] The dome is related to the baldachin or "four-poster," which may be considered a condensed image of the basic structure of existential space. As such it has been used throughout the history of ecclesiastical architecture to mark the symbolic center. Old St. Peter's, thus, had a baldachin over the altar, and the solution was repeated in a magnificent, typically Baroque fashion by Bernini 1300 years later.

Another double functioning figure which has served as a constituent element within the European city, is the *palazzo*, which externally appears as an enclosed, powerful block, and internally as a centralized courtyard. Since it originated as a domestic building, we shall discuss its basic phenomenology in the next chapter, but have to point out in this context that the *palazzo* when it acquires public significance, necessarily has to gain in formal precision and articulation.

Some of the typical figures which distinguish the historical cities have a simpler function, being restricted either to the exterior or to the interior

87. *The loss of the imago mundi: Kaiser Wilhelm-Gedächtniskirche, Berlin (E. Eiermann, 1957-63).*

88. *Notre-Dame du Haut, Ronchamp (Le Corbusier, 1953).*

89. *Unitarian Church, Rochester (L. Kahn, 1959).*

90. *Portland Building, Portland, Oregon (M. Graves, 1980).*

aspect. The tower and certain kinds of roofs, thus, mark points of focal interest, without themselves offering a corresponding explanatory interior. The cloister, on the contrary, is an important introvert figure which serves as a meaningful goal, without being prepared for by a conspicuous exterior. In many cities we also encounter elements possessing a strong figural quality which serve to mark the transition between exterior and interior. The portico (colonnade, arcade) is a well-known example. In some Italian cities it acquired the form of an independent *loggia* which acts as a civic symbol *per se*. The gateway is also a commonly used distinctive element which has been subject to various figural interpretations, from the Egyptian pylon and the Roman triumphal arch to the various types of city gates.[99]

Finally, we ought to mention the subordinate, variable *motifs* which usually characterize a settlement. External elements of this kind are first of all certain types of openings, such as portals and windows. Form, size and distribution determine their appearance. Gables, cornices and bases also belong to this category, as do certain kinds of wall treatment, such as rustication. Motifs are not figures in their own right, as they do not embody a total relationship between earth and sky, but they contribute to give the superior figures the necessary contact with concrete reality.

It ought to be repeated that the architectural figures mentioned above, are those objects of human identification which allow for public dwelling. They represent a common understanding of the world and stand forth as powerful images which make this understanding manifest. As landmarks, they also facilitate man's orientation.

Since the public building represents an institution of general value, it is less intimately related to the site than the domestic house. Architectural history, however, shows that the types of public architecture also vary in accordance with the locality. Towers, basilica facades and even interiors look different from city to city, although the basic qualities of the type are preserved. It is moreover important to notice that the influence of the *genius loci* remained, in spite of the changes determined by the various historical epochs.

Institution today

Modern architecture took the individual situation as its point of departure, rather than the common agreement. The symbolic types of the past were abolished and substituted by the functionalist credo that the forms should "follow from" the functions. As a result, public architecture tended towards simple efficiency, reducing for instance the city hall to an office building and the church to an assembly hall.[100]

Deprived of any meaningful explanation, man tended to lose his sense of belonging and fellowship, and the alienation caused by the insufficient possibilities of meeting offered by the modern city, was thereby enhanced. The "loneliness" of the inhabitant of the modern metropolis is in fact a much-discussed problem.

The shortcomings of modern public architecture were, however, soon recognized. Already in 1944 Giedion wrote an article with the title "The Need for a New Monumentality." Here he said: "Monumentality springs from the eternal need of people to create symbols for their activities and for their fate or destiny, for their religious beliefs and for their social convictions,"[101] and he

considered the "reconquest of monumental expression," the "third step," in the development of modern architecture, after the formation of the modern house and the restoration of urbanism. During the 1950s and 60s, however, the creation of symbolic forms got stuck in the impasse of neo-expressionism, which aimed at "exciting" effects rather than typological meaning. Although some of the buildings of the period were of high quality, such as Le Corbusier's church at Ronchamp or Scharoun's Philharmonie, neo-expressionism did not open up any path for further development.

An important turning point is however represented by the ideas and works of Louis Kahn. Kahn's famous question: "What does the building want to be?" poses the problem. A building wants to be some-thing. It is neither a "pattern" nor a "structure," but a thing which gathers a world. Thus it possesses an identity and a name. Kahn here returns to the "origins," in the sense of the basic modes of being in the world.[102]

Kahn's approach was taken as the point of departure for a whole generation of younger architects who wanted to reconquer the dimension of meaning in architecture. Their efforts are in several respects heterogeneous, but the common denominator is a renewed sense of the "grammar" of built form and organized space. A new public architecture is thus on the way, as is for instance proved by the recent works of Michael Graves.[103] Here archetypal forms reappear in new interpretations and combinations, offering the promise of an authentic figurative architecture. Modern architecture was a matter of principle "non-figurative," reducing form to abstract juxtapositions of abstract elements. What we need today is a return to the "powerful figures that build the world."

"Before he is thrown into the world," Bachelard writes, "man is put in the cradle of the house."[104] In the house man becomes familiar with the world in its immediacy; there he does not have to choose a path and find a goal, in the house and next to the house the world is simply given. We could also say that the house is the place where *daily life* takes place. Daily life represents what is continuous in our existence, and therefore supports us like a familiar ground. Why, then, do we have to throw ourselves into the world when we possess the cradle of the house? The answer is simply that the purposes of human life are not found at home; the role of each individual is part of a system of interactions which take place in a common world based on shared values. To participate we have to leave the house and choose a path. When our social task is accomplished, however, we withdraw to our home to recover our personal identity. Personal identity, thus, is the content of private dwelling.

What is the immediate world which is gathered and visualized by the house? It is simply the world of *phenomena*, as opposed to the public world of "explanations." Primarily, any phenomena is experienced as a *Stimmung* or atmosphere, that is, as a certain quality with which our "mood" or "state-of-mind" has to conform. Heidegger says: "The mood has already disclosed, in every case, Being-in-the-world as a whole, and makes it possible first of all to direct oneself towards something."[105] And Bollnow adds: "The mood is the simplest and most original form in which human life becomes aware of itself."[106] Together with mood, however, goes understanding, and an atmosphere is therefore always related to the recognition of things. "A state-of-mind always has its understanding," Heidegger says, and, "understanding always has its mood."[107] In the house this immediate and unified world of mood and understanding becomes present. The house, thus, does not offer understanding in the sense of explanation, but in the more original sense of "standing under" or among things. In the house man experiences his being part of the world.

How is this accomplished? Evidently the house has to keep and visualize the phenomena to make them accessible. The quality of light, for instance, varies from place, but it is difficult to grasp its varieties before it is made manifest by means of a built form. Thus Louis Kahn says: "The sun never knew how great it is before it struck the side of a building."[108] Many architects have understood that, and have designed windows which so to speak materialize light and thereby visualize the atmosphere of the place. Particularly beautiful is the bay-window in Mackintosh's Hill House near Glasgow (1912), where various perforated elements are added to the window proper, to reveal the rich nuances of Scottish light.

A house does not, however, only visualize the atmospheric qualities of the environment, it also ought to express the mood of the actions which take place inside. In the Hill House, thus, the entrance hall is characterized by an abundant use of stained wood, and a fireplace is found immediately inside the entrance door. An atmosphere of warm welcome and friendly shelter is thus created. The living room, on the contrary, celebrates light, not only by means of the above-mentioned window, but also through the use of colors and glazed tiles. It is hence experienced as a place with a liberating and festive character, suited for relaxed and inspiring togetherness. The main bedroom, finally, is distinguished by harmonious intimacy. The stylized flower motifs on the furniture give a subtle hint at fertility and procreation. The forms are in general softer here, and are unified visually and symbolically by the "celestial" vault over the marriage bed. Thus the Hill House makes a world of natural and human phenomena manifest in its varied immediacy. And this is the task of the house: to reveal the world, not as essence but as presence, that is, as material and color, topography and vegetation, seasons, weather and light. The Hill House shows that this revelation is achieved in two complementary ways: by opening up to the surrounding world and by offering a retreat from the same world. A retreat, however, is not a place where the outside world is forgotten; rather it is a place where man gathers his memories of the world and relates them to his daily life of eating, sleeping, conversation and entertainment. And a retreat is furthermore a place where the phenomena are condensed and emphasized to appear as "environmental forces." Thus Frank Lloyd Wright says to explain his use of the fireplace as the innermost core of the house: "It comforted me to see the fire burning deep in the masonry of the house."[109] We may in this connection also recall how the Glessner family in Chicago carried along the domestic fire from their old house, when they moved into the new one, designed by Richardson in 1885-86.

So far we have indicated the development of personal identity as the general purpose which determines the form of the house. The description of the Hill House, however, suggests that the life which takes place in the house primarily is a shared life. Withdrawal does not mean isolation, but rather a different kind of meeting, that is, the

91. The cradle of the house: The house of Carl Larsson in Sweden (1895).

intimate meeting of private dwelling. This meeting is based on love rather than understanding and agreement, and love in fact is the attitude which makes a direct contact with phenomena possible. The Swiss psychiatrist Binswanger, thus, defines the house as the space where "loving togetherness" takes place, and points out that the spatiality of love consists in "admittance" rather than "taking possession of."[110] We could also say that love is the basic state-of-mind which makes all the other moods possible.

The house is the fixed point which transforms an environment into a "dwelling place." The house gathers the chosen meanings which are intended by Wittgenstein, when saying: "I am my world." By means of the house we become friends with a world, and gain the foothold we need to act in it. As an architectural figure standing forth in the environment, the house confirms our identification and offers security. When we enter inside, we are finally "at home." In the house we find the things we know and cherish. We have brought them with us from the outside, and live with them because they represent "our world." We use them in our daily life, take them in our hands and enjoy their meaning as representations of *Erinnerungen*.[111] The interior therefore possesses the quality of interiority, and acts as a complement to our own inner self. When we thus realize private dwelling, we experience what is known as "domestic peace."

Morphology

From ancient times the house has been understood as a *microcosmos*. As a space within space it repeats the basic structure of the environment. The floor is the earth, the ceiling the sky, and the walls the encircling horizon. The etymology of the words floor, ceiling and

*93. Hill House, Helensburgh, bay-window
in the living room (C.R. Mackintosh, 1902).*

94. Hill House, entrance hall.   95. Hill House, bedroom.

wall confirms this interpretation. Any work of architecture, be it a public building or a house, is such an image of the world. The difference between the former and the latter, is that the public building visualizes the general properties of the environment, whereas the house presents it in its concrete immediacy. Vernacular architecture illustrates how that is done.

When we travel from Switzerland through the European continent up to Denmark, we encounter a series of houses which show an evident realtionship to their landscapes. The *châlet* of Simmental, thus, is distinguished by a large gable wall which opens towards the sun and the view with rows of glittering windows. The roof is not very pointed, and the general character is solid and ground-hugging, lending a sense of protection and assurance among the wild forms of the mountains. In nearby Emmental the mountains give way to rounded hills. Here the houses also have immense roofs, but they are steeper and half-hipped, so that the built form looks like a large, voluminous body. This type of roof is common in most of the hilly regions to the north and east of the Alps, and harmonizes well with the character of the landscape. In the Black Forest in Southwestern Germany we find a third major example of the Germanic *Einhaus*.[112] The Black Forest is also a hilly country, but the name shows that it is quite different from the fertile and smiling Emmental. Here the general form of the houses visualizes the somewhat sinister character of the environment, and the large and deep roof overhangs over the windows and balconies give the interior a kind of cave-like appearance. In Lower Saxony on the North German plains we also encounter the *Einhaus*. Everyone who has travelled through Westphalia,

Oldenburg or the northern Netherlands will remember how the broad, open landscape centers on the impressive volumes of the large farmhouses. With their long ridges surrounded by groups of trees, they look like man-made hills which give structure to the surroundings. Their form may be compared with the related but characteristically different roofs of the southern houses mentioned above. The northern house, however, indicates, through its pronounced direction and regular timber frame, an orthogonal organization of space which is absent in the south. In the Netherlands, in fact, where fields and canals form a grid, this organization is present in the environment itself. When we finally arrive in Denmark, we find a soft, rolling landscape with a small and intimate scale. Here the houses are low and inobtrusive under gentle, embracing roofs.

The relationship between house and landscape, however, is not only established by the overall form and the shape of the roof. It is also visualized by the use of materials and type of construction, and hence by the built form of the wall. In this context we can only point to the meaningful variations in the treatment of half-timbered construction from the "picturesque" framework of romantic Franconia to the regular grid of Lower Saxony. Very subtle environmental changes may be visualized in this way. We should, however, add a few words about the half-timbered townhouse. The gabled townhouse of Central Europe is undoubtedly one of the most characteristic and impressive manifestations of domestic architecture. Visually the gable faces the street, and the multijettied construction gives emphasis to the lively and strong appearance. The half-timbered towns are

distinguished by variety and unity; hardly two houses are alike, and still they all belong to the same "family." On the northern plains relatively simple and level wall surfaces are usual, whereas in the hilly country of central Germany the forms are livelier; steep gables, turrets and oriels contribute to the picturesque appearance.

In general, vernacular houses illustrate Heidegger's tenet that the buildings should "bring the inhabited landscape close to man." The landscape of vernacular architecture is the concrete landscape of daily life, and its characteristics are gathered and expressed by the houses in a direct and obvious way. Since visualization sometimes is assisted by complementation, however, this does not necessarily mean that the houses "look" like their surroundings. The principal means which are used, are the shaping of the roof and the articulation of the wall. In any case the qualities of the earth are of primary importance, whereas the sky is considered in a less direct way. The interior is usually conceived both as a continuation and a counterpoint to the surroundings. Continuation is in general achieved by means of natural materials, whereas furnishing, colors and decoration may add what the environment lacks, as in the Norwegian peasant cottage where rich floreal patterns remind of summer and fertility, and make it possible to survive the long, colorless winter psychologically. Vernacular architecture is intimately related to its environment, since the life it serves primarily consists in cultivating the land. It is therefore natural to ask whether urban and suburban houses show a similar relationship, or represent a more general interpretation of private dwelling. A basic difference obviously cannot exist, since the settlement as a whole ought to keep

and visualize the "inhabited landscape." The urban house, however, forms part of a social context, and therefore has to adapt more directly to its neighbors. The sub-urban dwelling, on the contrary, remains free from this restriction. Thus Alberti wrote: "...in Town you are obliged to moderate yourselves in several Respects according to the Privileges of your neighbor; whereas you have much more Liberty in the Country." Therefore "the Ornaments for the House in Town ought to be much more grave than those for a House in the Country, where all the gayest and most licentious Embellishments are allowable."[113] The difference pointed out by Alberti is emphasized by the fact that townhouses often contain more than one dwelling, and thus require an overall coordination of the elements. This does not, however, contradict the basic aim of visualizing the phenomena characteristic of the place. The townhouses of ancient cities such as Venice, Florence, Siena, Rome and Naples are in fact different, obviously because they represent a different given environment, although basic typological traits may be common.[114]

Also in the large townhouse, such as the Italian *palazzo*, we find that the treatment of the wall, and in particular the form, size and distribution of the openings, the upper termination and the material and color, serve to visualize given environmental characters, and thus to relate the building to an inhabited landscape.[115] In the townhouse, however, the relationship to the sky is usually more important than in vernacular buildings, whereas the presence of the earth is less felt. Thereby the townhouse becomes part of that general interpretation of the "between" of earth and sky which distinguishes any settlement. The for-

99. Peasant house from Lower Saxony.

100. The Knochenhaueramtshaus in Hildesheim (1529; destroyed 1945).

mal means employed are those of the public buildings, although in a less systematic and conspicuous way. In the townhouse *withdrawal* naturally has another meaning than out in the country. Here it implies the creation of an inner domain where the memories of the more distant environment are gathered. From ancient times the court-yard served as the core of this inner world of private dwelling. In the *palazzo* of the Renaissance and Baroque it was formalized to appear as an echo of that civilization to which the house belonged. A particularly splendid example is the *cortile* of Palazzo Farnese in Rome (1517 ff.) where a superimposition of classical orders makes the essence of natural and human phenomena manifest. A semi-public solution, thus, which indicates the integrated social system to which it belonged.

The great epoch of the sub-urban house started in the nineteenth century,[116] and in many countries it is still alive. As a broad generalization we may say that the built form of the suburban house recalls both its vernacular relatives and the more "civilized" townhouses. Thus it gathers a complex world of natural characters and circumstances, memories of the urban meeting, and dreams about the "good life." A multifarious content of this kind might easily lead to a superficial play with motifs, and in fact it did during the period of late nineteenth century historicism. If the content, however, is understood in terms of man's being between earth and sky, the result may be a signficant poetical statement, as is proved by Mackintosh's Hill House and its contemporaries: Saarinen's Hvitträsk near Helsinki (1902), Behrens' own house in Darmstadt (1901),[117] and Hoffmann's Palais Stocklet in Brussels (1905). A particularly interesting example is of-fered by Olbrich's *Dreihäusergruppe* in Darmstadt (1903) where three dwellings are built together and at the same time distinguished individually by "typical" gables: embracing, equilibrated and pointed. The phenomenological nature of the domestic built form here becomes manifest.

The suburban house was given a new interpretation by Frank Lloyd Wright. Or rather, Wright brought back to our attention the essential nature of the house as point of departure and retreat. Thus he opened up his plans to make them interact with the environment, at the same time as he created an inner world of protection and comfort. He himself characterized the house as a "broad shelter in the open."[118] To achieve this result he worked with planes parallel to the earth which make the building identify itself with the ground, in juxtaposition with vertical elements that direct space and fix it where needed. The core is always the large, erect chimney-stack, where the fire "is burning deep in the masonry of the house itself."

We understand, thus, that Wright's "destruction of the box" did not contradict the idea of house, but rather opened up for authentic private dwelling in our time.

Topology

Because of the differentiated functions of daily life, the paths and goals of the house produce more complex patterns than those of the public building. The house, thus, is less "formal," although it constitutes a spatial organism. Again we find that the three basic principles of organization determine the possible solutions. Centralized and axial plans have been convincingly used throughout history, whereas the simple cluster may be considered a less convincing alternative. The origin of the central-ized plan is undoubtedly the court-house of the Near East and the Mediterranean countries.[119] It has been in use up till the present day, both in the form of a low one-family structure and a multi-story block of flats. In the court-house the center is the common, "social" room, around which the more special functions are gathered. In most cases the layout is not strictly symmetrical, and only aims at a general sense of enclosure. The Popeian atrium house represents the apex of the court-house. In *Vers une Architecture* Le Corbusier recognizes its importance: "Again the little vestibule which frees your mind from the street. And then you are in the Atrium; four columns in the middle shoot up towards the shade of the roof, giving a feeling of force and a witness of potent methods, but at the far end is the brilliance of the garden seen through the peristyle which spreads out this light with a large gesture, distributes it and accentuates it, stretching widely from left to right, making a great space. Between the two is the Tablinum, contracting this vision like the lens of a camera. On the right and on the left two patches of shade — little ones. Out of the clatter of the swarming street which is for every man and full of picturesque incidents, you have entered the house of a *Roman*."[120]

A nordic parallel to the court-house is represented by the hall-house, where a common room is again placed at the center, here however closed off by a ceiling. The solution, which goes back to the Middle Ages, is evidently determined by the climate, and by the demand for a space where family life may take place. Thus Baillie Scott writes: "(The hall) ...is to be a room where the family can meet together — a general gathering-place with its large fireplace and ample floor space... Whether it is called hall, houseplace, or living room,

some such apartment is a necessary feature as a focus to the plan of the house."[121] The other rooms of the house "may be considered as subsidiary to the central dominating room, and in some cases some of these may take the form of recesses in it."[122] What Baillie Scott here advocates, is an alternative to the clustering of separate small boxes within a large box, which was the most usual way of planning a house at this time. His conception is related to that of Frank Lloyd Wright. Not only do both architects oppose the "box," but they also introduce a double-height common room as the spatial focus of the house. Furthermore both stress the importance of the fireplace as the innermost core. "...a house, however warm, without a fire may be compared to a summer day without the sun," Baillie Scott writes.[123] What is different, however, is Wright's insistence upon opening up the rooms towards the environment, to satisfy the other basic aim of the house: the gathering of the phenomena of the site. To accomplish that, he had to combine his "centralized" shelter with a set of active directions.

Directed plans have also been legion during the course of history. In smaller houses of the *Megaron* type, the direction is simply a matter of axial symmetry, whereas in larger ones it may be marked by a passage onto which rooms are added on either side. The passage usually leads to a goal, be it a major room or a veranda. We find this basic layout in vernacular houses as well as suburban villas. Sometimes the direction of movement is parallel to the direction of the house itself, as in the *Einhaus* of Lower Saxony. But often it runs across the main volume to connect its two sides. This is for instance the case in the villas and garden palaces of the Baroque, where an axis joins the

urban *cour d'honneur* to the garden on the other side, integrating usually on its way a large staircase and a *sala terrena*. Recently the directed plan has been revived by several post-modern architects.[124]

Although the spatial organization of a house is necessarily less systematic than that of a public building, it may possess a conspicuous figural quality. The courtyard, the hall, the passage and the veranda (or porch) are distinct figures which transform the domestic space into a place where life may take place. Private dwelling, thus, does not consist in a withdrawal into a formless nowhere, but demands a defined and imageable stage. "The empty stage of a room is fixed in space by boundaries; it is animated by light, organized by focus and liberated by outlook," we read in *The Place of Houses* by Moore, Allen and Lyndon.[125]

The event of modern architecture contributed significantly to the development of domestic typology. Wright's "destruction of the box" and the resulting "free plan" broke with the conventional use of paths and goals, in terms of passages and enclosed halls. Instead, space was intended as a "flowing" continuum without clearly defined zones. The general aim was to make man feel "at home" in the modern, open world.[126] Thus Moholy-Nagy wrote: "A dwelling should not be a retreat from space, but life *in* space."[127] Wright therefore created a centrifugal plan, which represented a new interpretation of the concept of refuge. Rather than a retreat, the house became a fixed point in space, from which man could experience a new sense of freedom and participation. This point is marked by the great fireplace. Wright's re-interpretation of the human dwelling remains one of the most significant achievements in the

history of modern architecture. "Behind the whole development of free design was the insistent belief that man must live as a free human being, in close contact with nature, in order to realize his own potentialities," Scully writes, and "America consequently produced her most original monuments where one would after all have expected to find them: in the homes of individual men."[128] During the following development, however, the free plan degenerated into a kind of general unidentifiable openness, making alienation rather than freedom manifest. Thus we recognize the eternal need for spatial figures which tell us where we are.

Typology
Due to the multifarious ways of daily life and the infinitely varied local conditions, the typology of the house is much more complex than that of public architecture. And still we all know that house types exist. It is sufficient to travel through any European region to realize that. In this context we shall only single out some fundamental examples which have recurred during the course of history.

In ancient Rome two kinds of domestic structures were created which should come to play an important role in the history of architecture, the *domus* and the *insula*, that is, the atrium or peristyle house and the urban tenement house.[129] The first is the prototype which initiated the development of the villa and the suburban house in southern Europe, and the second was the point of departure for the urban block, known from most Western cities. Being court-houses, both have a conspicuous figural quality as regards space. The domus, however, does not appear as an identifiable unit when seen from the outside. This relative anonymity of the single house within

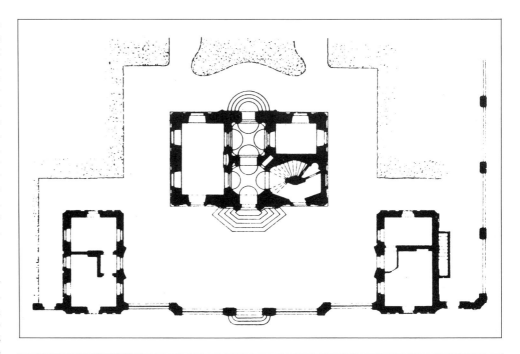

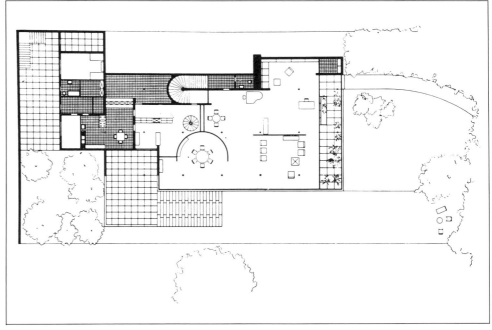

the urban matrix is characteristic of the Mediterranean countries, where the "home" never gained the same importance as an object of identification as in the cold North. The saying "my home is my castle" does not apply to Italy, where private dwelling is subordinate to the social life of the *piazza*. What we have called "daily life" here takes place outdoors, whereas the house of a certain standing rather serves a representative semi-public purpose. This fact is proved by the formal layout of the main interior spaces (atrium, cortile, salone), as well as the symmetrical order of the palazzo facade. All the same, the domus and the insula allowed for withdrawal, a value which was needed to escape from the noise of the traffic in the crowded streets.

During the Middle Ages, and namely in Central and Western Europe, two other types of constituent importance developed: the hall-house and the row house. Both were in general conceived as gabled structures which appear as distinct figures in relation to their surroundings. The basic image of the nordic house, thus, is determined by the steep, pitched roof. The origin of this form is most significant, and tells us how the house has gained a meaning which goes beyond its mere utilitarian purpose. The gabled house stems from a simple post-and-beam construction, which in its primitive form consisted of two posts carrying a ridge beam from which roofs sloped down to the ground on either side. The gabled ends of the posts gave the name to the structure, or rather, to its appearance as a built form. Jost Trier has shown that this simple structure was considered a model of the world. That is, the house became a means to understand the world; its structure was so to speak projected into the between of earth and

sky. "The gable shows how the house conquers the space of the sky. The ridge is the celestial axis... the gables at its ends are the heavenly poles... the posts are the *universalis columna quasi sustiens omnia*."[130] The world, hence, was understood as a large house, as something built, ordered and articulated. And thereby the house helped man to dwell, not only in the house itself, but in the world at large. It is important, however, to emphasize that this function of the house does not correspond to the explanation offered by the public building. Whereas the public building gathers a complex totality into a generalized symbol, the house was understood as a concrete *replica* of the world, that is, as a representation of what is immediately given. We may conclude that the house and the public building have a common origin and stem from man's primeval need for finding an existential foothold. In the house the original form of understanding is preserved, whereas the public building represents a higher level of generalization.

The intimate relationship of the house to what is immediately given, makes it become the constituent element of the general background to human life, and thereby conditions its mood. It *is* so to speak "life," whereas the public building is "idea." When the basic types of house are repeated, this background becomes manifest as an extented matrix which supports daily life. The repetition, however, is not a mechanical one. Rather it consists in what we have called "theme and variations." Domestic architecture was always based on this principle. In the matrix of houses, figures appear, disappear and reappear like the motifs of musical polyphony, reflecting thus the transcience and recurrence of phenomena.

Our reference to the basic types of the South and the North has suggested that the themes of different localities are not the same. In the "classical" South, thus, the world is immediately given as something built and ordered, and man does not need the help of the structured house to come to terms with it. Hence the "neutral," volumetric form of the southern house, which only serves to offer a permanent "here." As a result, the domestic matrix becomes a general background to the distinct and conspicuous public buildings, which reveal the properties of the given order. In the "romantic" North, on the contrary, the world is complex and changing and distinguished by a multitude of incomprehensible nuances. To understand this world, the general explanation of public architecture is not sufficient; here man also needs an image which offers security in his daily life. That is, he needs a house which is simultaneously refuge and opening on the world. The domestic matrix therefore gains in importance, and the public structures appear as the most significant variations on common themes, rather than as individual monuments. The medieval cities of Central and Western Europe with their "family" of pointed gables and church spires illustrate that.

In the house our wandering has come to an end. We have experienced the forces and forms of the landscape, have approached the settlement as a place of arrival, and have been excited by the meeting and possibilities offered by urban space. We have also discovered the facade of the public building and been invited by its promise. After having received the explanation inside and gained a foothold in a shared world, we have withdrawn into our house, where the world is again present in its immediacy. And still, the world of the house is different from the world outside. What was *given* there, is here under-stood and *er-lebt*. Thus the house brings the inhabited landscape close to man, and thus it becomes the cradle from where we can start our wandering again.

House today
The modern movement took the creation of a *new dwelling* as its point of departure. "The present development in building is undoubtedly focused on the dwelling, and in particular on the dwelling for the *common man...* Neither the public building nor the factory is today of equal importance. That means: we are again concerned about the human being," Giedion wrote in 1929.[131] Already in 1925 at the Exposition Internationale des Arts Décoratifs in Paris, Le Corbusier showed a prototype apartment, which he called the *Pavillon de l'esprit nouveau*. Thus he did not demonstrate the "spirit" of the modern age by means of a monumental symbol, but with a dwelling for the common man. We may also recall his words: "Human beings are badly housed, that is the profound and real reason for the present upheavals."[132] We have already referred to the pioneering effort of Frank Lloyd Wright in solving the problem of the new dwelling, and may add that his works became a major source of inspiration to European architects after their publication in Germany in 1910. During the twenties and thirties, thus, the modern house and the modern flat were developed, and undoubtedly represented a significant contribution to the improvement of man's living conditions.[133]

And still, the modern house could not fully satisfy the needs of private dwelling. What was lacking, was simply what we have called "figural quality." The modern house was certainly prac-

tical and healthy, but *it did not look like a house*. In fact, it favored "life in space" rather than "life with images." When modern houses became numerous, this was felt as a lack, and the demand for "meaningful" forms came up. Robert Venturi's work must be understood in this context. Thus he reintroduced "conventional" elements such as gables and arches, and aimed at giving his houses the identity of a "tower," a "garden pavilion" or a "balcony on the world." "If the facade at Chestnut Hill was a child's two-dimensional image of a house, here the image expands to three dimensions, for what is basic here is the sense one has

of this building as an object, tall and wooden, sitting among the trees in its lush semi-rural site," Paul Goldberger writes about the Carl Tucker House.[134]

The problem of figural quality, however, is not only a question of visual images. It is also related to the demand for *places* where daily life may take place. This problem has been treated recently by Charles Moore, Gerald Allen and Donlyn Lyndon in the above-mentioned book *The Place of Houses*, and in numerous dwellings built in collaboration with William Turnbull and Richard Whitaker. In their solutions the spatial figures of the

house are given a new interpretation. Centrifugal movement is thus expressed by peripherally added rooms "like saddlebags," whereas the center itself is emphasized through the introduction of a baldachin or "four-poster." Interacting zones are moreover defined by the insertion of perforated vertical "shafts" in a generally open space.[135]

The examples show that a reconquest of figural quality is on the way, relating the here and now to the there and then. In many post-modern dwellings, in fact, we again encounter the archetypal forms of the house and enjoy their inexhaustible possibilities of ever new figural manifestations.

VI. Language

The four modes of dwelling have a common denominator: *language.* "Language is the house of Being," Heidegger says, intending that language contains the whole of reality.[136] What does that mean? What does the word "house" mean here? It means that everything that is, is known through language, and that everything remains in language. Things and language are given together. We all know the strange experience of meeting something or somebody without yet knowing the name. It is the name which makes what is perceived part of a world, and hence makes it a meaningful percept. "In the naming, the things named are called into their thinging." Therefore language is the "house" of Being. Man's being-in-the-world as mood and understanding depends on language, or, in Heidegger's words: "Discourse is existentially equiprimordial with state-of-mind and understanding."[137] No world is given without language, and in language the world is, so to speak, stored. When man speaks, he makes what is kept in language appear. In speaking, he reveals how things are, rather than expressing "himself." Therefore Heidegger says: "Language speaks, ...and, "man speaks only as he responds to language."[138]

Heidegger's understanding of language differs fundamentally from the current linguistic theory which considers language a system of conventional signs, or "code."[139] This theory deprives language of any existential basis, and reduces it to an arbitrary, "culturally determined" construct, which serves communication rather than revelation. Language evidently *is* a means of communication and *has* a historical dimension; this, however, does not explain its fundamental nature as the "house of Being." It

follows from Heidegger's definition that discourse is a "putting into words" of *truth,* which, in accordance with the Greek concept of *alétheia,* happens as simultaneous disclosure and concealment. That is, when something is revealed, it implies that other aspects of what *is,* remain hidden. We can never have the whole truth, but only illuminate certain aspects at a time. This process never stops, and the way it happens is certainly culturally determined. It takes place, however, within the "house of Being," which is always there as the timeless ground on which revelation occurs. When man speaks, he founds this ground and at the same time relates what is transcient to what remains, giving it thus its "measure."[140]

How, then, does man speak? "Poetry speaks in images," Heidegger says, and "poetry is what really lets us dwell."[141] That is, when man speaks he creates an image which reveals the world, and offers us an existential foothold. Such images disclose the nature of things as interdependent parts of that "mirror-play" which is the world. "Earth and sky, divinities and mortals... each of the four mirrors in its own way the presence of the others... This mirroring does not portray a likeness. The mirroring, lightening each of the four, appropriates their own presencing into simple belonging to one another... This appropriative mirroring sets each of the four free into its own, but it binds these free ones into the simplicity of their essential being toward one another."[142] Thus "the poet calls all the brightness of the sights of the sky and every sound of its courses and breezes into the singing word and there makes them shine and ring. Yet the poet, if he is a poet does not describe the mere appearance of sky and earth. The poet calls, in the

sights of the sky, that which in its very self-disclosure causes the appearance of that which conceals itself, and indeed *as* that which conceals itself.[143] Thus the image lets the invisible be seen, and lets man dwell. What is here stated, is that poetry is the authentic mode of discourse, and that all other uses of language are made possible by poetic understanding. "Poetry proper is never merely a higher mode of everyday language. It is rather the reverse: Everyday language is a forgotten and used-up poem."[144]

It goes without saying that language is *shared.* As the "house of Being" it is not invented individually, but given as part of a common world. Thus it does not only help man to belong to the earth, but also to belong to the others. Being-in-the-world is always a being-with-others[145] and to share a world is not only a question of the here and now but of the common ground.

The language of architecture
To be able to understand the language of architecture, it has been necessary to look into the nature of language in general. How, then is architecture a language? Evidently buildings do not name anything, they are not words and it is even doubtful whether they may be considered "signs."[146] And still, they speak. Over and over again those who have been open to listen, have beheld the "saying" of works of architecture. "Few things are indeed so strange as this thaumaturgic art of the builder," Baillie Scott writes, "he places stones in certain positions — cuts them in certain ways, and behold, they begin to speak with tongues — a language of their own, with meanings too deep for words.[147] When this happens, truth is not "put into words," but rather "set into work." It is not enough that man

"says" the things, he also has to keep and visualize them in concrete images which help us to see our environment as it is. Together with painting, sculpture, and music, Heidegger explicitly names architecture as one of the arts which "in essence are poetry." In general, "art is the setting-into-work of truth."[148] Basically this happens as a "poetic projection" which "sets itself into work as figure (Gestalt)." "Figure is the structure in whose shape the rift composes and submits itself.[149] The world "rift" (*Riss*) here means the difference between thing and world, that is, between beings and Being. In "composing the rift," things are illuminated and world revealed. The word "figure" does not mean an abstract shape but a concrete embodiment. "The rift must set iself back into the heavy weight of stone, the dumb hardness of wood, the dark glow of colors."[150] In general, embodiment takes place in things, or in the "earth," which Heidegger in this context understands as the opposite of world. The setting-into-work thus becomes as "strife between world and earth," the world offering the "measure" and the earth the "boundary" of the figure.

To illustrate his notion of art, Heidegger uses an example taken from architecture. "A building, a Greek temple, portrays nothing. It simply stands there in the middle of the rock-cleft valley. The building encloses the figure of the god, and in this concealment lets it stand out into the holy precinct through the open portico... The temple and its precinct, however, do not fade away into the indefinite. It is the templework that fits together and at the same time gathers around itself the unity of those paths and relations in which birth and death, disaster and blessing, victory and disgrace, endurance and decline acquire the shape

of destiny for the human being... Standing there, the building rests on the rocky ground. This resting draws up out of the rock the mystery of that rock's clumsy yet spontaneous support. Standing there, the building holds its ground against the storm raging above it and so first makes the storm manifest in its violence. The luster and gleam of the stone, though itself apparently glowing only by the grace of the sun, yet first brings to light the light of the day, the breadth of the sky, the darkness of the night. The temple's firm towering makes visible the invisible space of air.. The temple-work, standing there, opens up a world and at the same time sets this world back again on earth, which itself only thus emerges as native ground... The temple, in its standing there, first gives to things their look and to men their outlook on themselves."[151]

What does this passage tell us? To begin with Heidegger points out that the work of art, the building, does not represent anything; rather it *presents*: it brings something into presence. Then he goes on telling what this something is. First, the temple makes the god present. Second, it "fits together" what shapes the destiny of human being. Finally, the temple makes all the things of the earth visible: the rock, the sea, the air, the plants, the animals, and even the light of the day and the darkness of the night. In doing this, the temple "opens up a world and at the same time sets this world back again on earth." Thus it sets truth into work. How, then, is that accomplished? Four times Heidegger repeats that the temple does what it does by "standing there." Both words are important. The temple does not stand anywhere; it stands *there*, "in the middle of the rock-cleft valley." The words rock-cleft valley are certain-

119. The column between earth and sky: second
Hera temple, Paestum (fifth century B.C.).

120. Composition: the Colosseum, Rome (86).

ly not introduced as an ornament. Rather they indicate that temples are built in particular, prominent places. By means of the building the place gets extension and delimitation, whereby a holy precinct is formed. In other words, the meaning of the place is revealed by the building. How the building makes the destiny of the people present, is not explicit, but it is implied that this is done simultaneously with the housing of the god, which means that the fate of the people is also intimately related to the place. The visualization of the earth, finally, is taken care of by the temple's standing. It *rests* on the ground and *towers* into the air. In doing this, it gives to things their look. In general, the temple is not "added" to the place as something foreign, but, standing there, first makes the place emerge as what it is. What a poem and a work of art have in common is their being images, or in our terminology, their *figural quality*. A work is in addition a thing; but a thing as such does not possess the quality of image. As a gathering it mirrors the fourfold in its way, but its thingness is hidden and has to be disclosed by the work. Thus Heidegger shows how Van Gogh's painting of a pair of peasant shoes reveal the thingness of the shoes. By themselves, the shoes are mute, but the work of art speaks for them. Thus the work gives the world presence.

We have already, following Heidegger, defined the world which is disclosed by the work of architecture as the known or "inhabited" landscape. We have also pointed out that the spatiality of this landscape may be understood in terms of the two aspects, admittance and embodiment. A location, thus, makes room for the fourfold and simultaneously, as a built thing, discloses the fourfold. Evidently a work of architecture does not make a total world visi-

ble, but only certain of its aspects. These aspects are contained in the concept of spatiality. Spatiality is a concrete term denominating a domain of things which constitute an inhabited landscape. The Greek example in fact starts with the image of a rock-cleft valley and later refers to several concrete elements of earth and sky. But it also suggests that landscape cannot be isolated from human life and from the divine. The inhabited landscape therefore is a manifestation of the fourfold, and comes into presence through the buildings which bring it close to man. We could also say that the inhabited landscape denominates the spatiality of the fourfold. This spatiality becomes manifest as a particular *between* of earth and sky, that is, as a *place*. A work of architecture is therefore not an abstract organization of space. It is a concrete figure, where the plan (*Grundriss*) mirrors the admittance, and the elevation (*Aufriss*) the embodiment. Thus it brings the inhabited landscape close, and lets man dwell poetically, which is the ultimate aim of architecture.

In the last four chapters we have discussed the morphology, topology and typology of the manifestations of the modes of dwelling, and should to conclude sum up the findings in some general remarks on the language of architecture.

Morphology

We have acknowledged that the meaning of a built form consists in its standing, rising and opening, that is, in its being between earth and sky. Through its being between earth and sky it gathers and embodies a world. We may also say that the embodiment takes place in the boundaries which define the spaces where life takes place, primarily in the *wall*. Thus we have

discussed the wall of the settlement, the wall of the urban spaces, the wall of the public building and the wall of the house, and found that they are distinguished by certain characteristics. The city wall, thus, mainly appears as a silhouette, the urban wall as a varied repetition of a "theme," the public wall as a conspicuous order, and the private wall as a relatively informal reflection of a particular "here." We have also mentioned that floor and ceiling (roof) play a role in the definition of the built form. In vernacular architecture, thus, the roof usually recalls the forms of the landscape, whereas the public roof may act as a symbolic landmark, for instance in the shape of a dome.[152]

The wall is as a matter of fact composed of elements. Thus it usually consists of stories which are more or less distinguished from each other. This distinction is taken care of by means of subordinate elements such as columns, architraves, arches, windows, bases and cornices. Together these elements constitute a built figure. What, then, is in this context the difference between element and figure? The figure is characterized by being a form which gathers earth and sky. The three-story wall of the "classical" palace may illustrate what this means. The ground-floor should at the same time express closeness to the earth, that is, solidity and enclosure, and entry, that is, communication with the outside world. This double and, in a certain sense, contradictory task, has for instance been solved by means of mighty stone piers, possibly in connection with squat arches. Magnificent examples are found in the buildings of Richardson and Sullivan.[153] The top floor, on the contrary, should present closeness to the sky and a panoramic view. It was therefore often transformed into a light and open *loggia* or *belvedere*. The *piano nobile* in-between, finally, is the level where human encounter takes place, and is therefore characterized by anthropomorphic columns or pilasters, or by windows with classical surrounds. Thus the wall as a whole makes the between of earth and sky manifest. The single stories, however, as well as the transitions: base, string course and cornice, are not figures. Rather they are "elements," which relate up and down, and therefore only gain their full meaning when they are "composed." A column is also a figure. It keeps earth and sky apart and relates them to each other. But the base and the capital are not figures. A capital does not fully relate earth and sky if it is taken out of its context. An architrave belongs primarily to the earth, whereas a pediment relates earth and sky and thus possesses figural quality. An element may, however, sometimes become a quasi-figure because of its characteristic form, which, when perceived, makes us remember the totality to which it belongs. The keystone is a well-known example.

The composition of elements usually depends on a comprehensive "vision," that is, on an imagined figure which determines the solution. It also follows certain general principles which, in their turn, depend on the structure of existential spatiality. First, any composition has to take the difference between horizontality and verticality into consideration, and conceive the figure in terms of rhythm and tension, or, in short, proportions. Thus the wall may "tell" about the life it is related to, as horizontal admittance of actions and vertical embodiment of characters. Second, the composition ought to be hierarchical, as any situation consists of superior and subordinate elements. A main entrance, thus, is more important than a window within a row, and

a columnar order is more important than the background on which it appears. One of the reasons why so many buildings from the historicist period at the end of the nineteenth century appear so confusing, is in fact that all parts are given the same importance.[154] Third, the composition ought to possess structural identity, real or fictitious.[155] Thus it has to be conceived as being massive or skeletal, or a combination of both. A built form always has a structural "basis," since the structure as such brings forth the relationship between up and down, namely by expressing the force of gravity. Architectural history in fact demonstrates that there has always been a correspondence between form and technique, although the latter often has been fake. We may in this context recall that Serlio called massive rustication *opera di natura* and the classical skeleton *opera di mano*. Thus the two basic types of construction as such reveal aspects of the world.

Our discussion of the boundaries of settlements, urban spaces, buildings and houses has shown that the composition of the wall expresses what the totality it belongs to "wants to be." Thus we do not find a direct similarity between the different parts of a settlement. And still, they somehow belong to the same "family." This shows that a certain way of being between earth and sky may be expressed in more general as well as particular terms. In Prague, for instance, "all" buildings are distinguished by being simultaneously ground-hugging and soaring. In the houses this double character is suggested by solid bases and picturesque roofs crowned by dormers, in the public buildings, namely the churches, it becomes an intensely emphasized expression which is achieved by means of horizontal bands of rustication down on the ground and

119

125. *Fictitious structure: S. Maria delle Carceri, Prato (G. da Sangallo, 1484).*

fantastic spires up in the air.[156] Thus the settlement appears as a unified, albeit differentiated, whole, and man's identification may become a continuous living process. Such local characteristics often reflect the vernacular architecture of the region, and prove Heidegger's words that "the dialect is the mysterious source of any mature language."[157]

The basic characteristics which unite the different parts of a settlement constitute a local "style." In addition to such limited styles, however, the language of architecture also comprises general styles, which, during the course of history, have moved from place to place, and proved to be valid "everywhere." The outstanding example is the classical language, which has not only been assimilated in the most different places, but also kept alive down to our time. The reason is evidently that the classical orders disclose basic natural and human characters and moreover bring the two into a meaningful relationship.[158] Therefore classical architecture only had to be subject to minor modifications to adapt to the local conditions of the places where it was taken into use. The success of classical architecture is also due to the fact that it constitutes a "complete" system, which comprises all the basic parts of a building as well as generalized elements which may be used in ever new combinations and through articulation embody any character. Architectural history in fact illustrates the infinite possibilities of the classical language, from Antiquity through the Renaissance and the Baroque to the various neoclassical currents of the last two centuries.

In general, the language of architecture serves to give the built form figural quality. Figural quality does not consist in exciting inventions, but in

126. Auditorium Building, Chicago,
(Adler and Sullivan, 1887).

127. "Opera di natura, opera di mano,"
Palazzo Montecitorio, Rome (Bernini, 1650).

128. Street in Prague with St. Nicholas
(K.I. Dientzenhofer 1739-51).

the manifestation of basic relationships between earth and sky. We may distinguish between four such relationships. First, a built form may be set off towards both the earth and the sky by clearly defined elements. This is the classical solution, as exemplified by the podium and the cornice of the Greek temple. Second, the form may have a "free" termination both below and above. This is the romantic solution, as exemplified by many medieval castles and by modern "organic" buildings. Third, the form may have a clear base but terminate freely towards the sky. This is the relationship characteristic of Prague, but also of Utzon's "platform" architecture. Forth, the form may grow freely out of the ground but have a simple and straight upper termination. This is a solution much used in the "romantic classicism" of the Nordic countries, as well as in some modern buildings, such as Le Corbusier's La Tourette. In all four cases the human between becomes part of a meaningful figural theme which defines a way of being between earth and sky.

In general, the built form has to be combined with an organized space to constitute an architectural figure. Sometimes, however, it appears as a figure in its own right, for instance as a facade within an urban context.

Topology

Spatial organization implies the composition of spatial elements. A spatial element may be any kind of enclosure, delimited by built or suggested boundaries. To become part of a composition, however, it has to possess a defined form of its own. Its plan may for instance be a square, a rectangle, a circle or an oval. Such geometrical units do not only have a defined outline, they also contain an invisible "structural

skeleton" of centers and axes which make it possible to join them "organically" together.[159] An organizing axis, thus, is not always superimposed on the plan, but may belong to the spatial elements themselves, and a center is not necessarily introduced as a "foreign" feature, but is potentially already there as part of the structural skeleton. Since any geometrical form contains axes which run in several directions, the possibility of composition are numerous. To make spatial organization more intelligible, the axes are sometimes marked in the floor. An emphasis of this kind may be particularly important when the spatial elements are topological, and the axes therefore are "suggested" rather than part of the form.

A spatial element is not only determined by its plan, but also by the section. A flat ceiling does not influence the shape which is indicated by floor and walls, whereas a barrel vault or a dome reveals the "hidden" axis or center. In the past changes in the treatment of the ceiling were often used to identify or interconnect the spatial elements and zones, a possibility which was mostly lost when modern architecture advocated the exclusive use of flat planes. A succession of variously defined spaces make a rhythm manifest which admits certain actions, at the same time as the section indicates characterizing tensions.

The composition of spatial elements in general makes use of two basic methods, which have been denominated "addition" and "division."[160] While the buildings of the Renaissance may be understood as an addition of relatively independent spatial elements, the Baroque deprived the parts of their independence by giving them a form which appears meaningless in isolation. In Baroque architecture the totality is so to speak given in advance and "divided" afterwards. It is, however, also possible to make the elements which participate in a spatial row or group interdependent, for instance by letting them alternately contract and expand, a method we have encountered in the works of Borromini, Guarini and their followers. Another possibility is to make two distinct elements interpenetrate, whereby an ambiguous zone is formed which at the same time belongs to both elements. We also know wholes which exhibit a certain articulation, but where it is difficult or impossible to recognize the elements. In this case we should talk about "fusion." It seems therefore right to expand the concept of "division" to include "pulsation," "interpenetration" and "fusion," and to group them all under the heading "integration."[161]

The methods of spatial composition serve as an indispensable tool which helps us to understand the nature of existing works of architecture, and thus the existential space they concretize. When we for instance notice that classical Greek layouts such as Delphi and Olympia consist of an addition of separate buildings, we recognize the wish for symbolizing individual characters. The single temple thus appears as a distinct member of a "family," just as the gods formed a family which symbolized the various roles and interactions of men on earth. In Roman architecture, on the contrary, a strong wish for spatial integration is evident, which visualizes an understanding of the world as an ordered cosmos. In the Renaissance the cosmos was interpreted in terms of homogeneous, tri-dimensional geometry, and accordingly buildings and layouts were conceived as an addition of elementary spatial "cells." Homogeneous space was a fundamentally new image, which, for the first time in architectural history, allowed for formal integration of the different environmental levels. Whereas the Romans applied the symbolic motif of the intersecting axes to all levels without, however, arriving at the concept of a spatial continuum, Renaissance space is basically the same on all levels. The concept of homogeneity was a point of departure for the Baroque "vitalization" of space, where the different parts are simultaneously differentiated and integrated, forming the extended, pulsating organisms referred to above.

The "free plan" of modern architecture also took the concept of homogeneity as its point of departure, but in contrast to the Baroque introduction of centers and axes which determine interacting zones, the free plan is based on division. That is, the given, infinite continuum is subdivided by free-standing partitions which direct the spatial flow. An open, dynamic world is thus visualized, where dwelling becomes "life in space" rather than the choice of a known place. Evidently the concept of total spatial openness cannot satisfy the four modes of dwelling. We have seen that urban space depends on enclosure and the space of public buildings on a regular, "explanatory" composition. The free plan was in fact developed in connection with the house, where open informality represents a valid alternative. Even here, however, the free plan could not satisfy the need for defined places. A return to spatial organisms based on the principles of addition and integration is therefore on the way. An interesting proposal in this context is represented by Paolo Portoghesi's interpretation of architectural space as a system of interacting "fields" generated by cen-

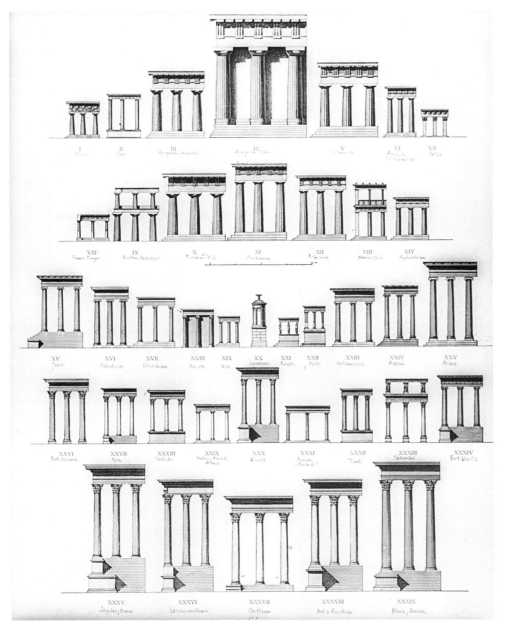

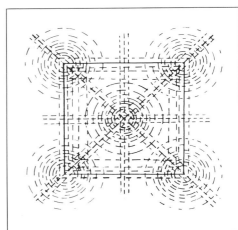

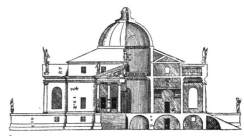

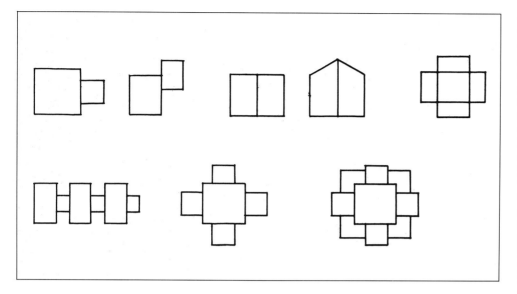

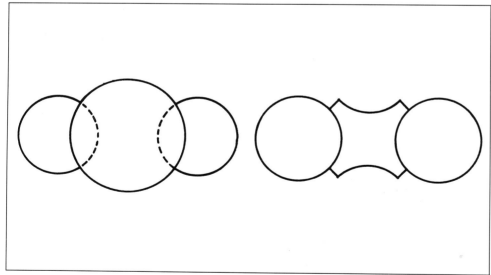

ters which gather the external and internal "forces." When the fields interact, zones of varying density and dynamism are created, which allow a complex life to take place.[162] The method may be considered a further development of Baroque integration, at the same time as valuable properties of the free plan are preserved.

By means of the methods of spatial composition, figures are formed which facilitate man's orientation in the environment. From what has been said, we understand that "orientation" not only means to find one's way about, but also to experience space as consisting of a set of interrelated, meaningful places. This experience presupposes that the environment consists of distinct spatial figures. Any place on any level has to possess figural quality, not only as a built form, but also as a void which admits life and makes an image of the spatiality of the world manifest. In our discussion of urban, public and private space, we have mentioned some of these figures and related them to the basic properties of path and goal. The additional remarks on elements and composition have indicated that a spatial figure has to possess formal identity in terms of a regular "structural skeleton."

Typology

A spatial organization does not become a place before it is set into work by means of a built form. The typical figures which constitute the substantives of the language of architecture, therefore may be defined as spatial figures possessing concrete boundaries. The spatial figure as such is a "volume"; when it is set into work, however, it becomes a building with a defined character. To set into work means to make a way of being between earth and sky manifest. Thus a building

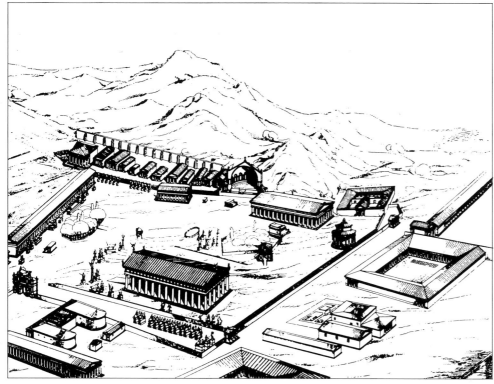

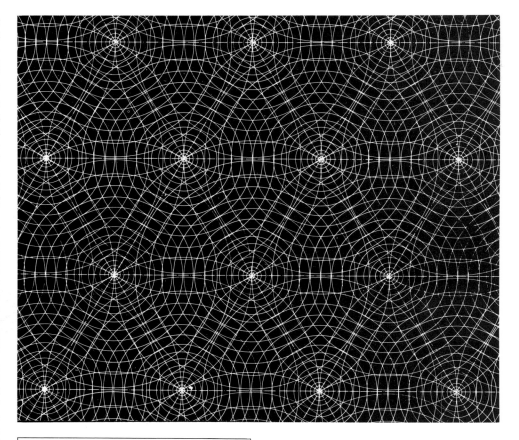

may stand up in space, stretch out or enclose a space, at the same time as it opens up in various ways. We have already pointed out that our language has names for such "beings": "tower," "block," "wing," "hall," "passage" and "dome." A tower is not simply an abstract vertical, but a thing that stands and rises. A wing is not just a horizontal, but a thing that lies and extends on the ground. A hall is not only a volume, but a room which relates down and up, and a dome is a form which recalls the immaterial vaulting sky over the solid earth.

The figures may be simple or composite; the Baptistry in Florence, thus, is an elementary, albeit conspicuous figure, whereas the adjacent cathedral is composite. The latter in fact combines hall, dome and tower into one complex but distinct totality. In the past our environment consisted of simple and composite figures. The built matrix of the houses was in general made up of simple figural units, whereas the public buildings presented more articulate compositions acting as landmarks and spatial foci. We may compare with the old-fashioned wooden buildings blocks of children, whose simple figural elements could be lined up or composed to form more complex wholes. The Froebel games used by Frank Lloyd Wright during his childhood were of this kind, and it is interesting to know that the resulting structures were supposed to get a name: "farm," "barge," "newsstand"...[163] A *concrete*, figural approach to architecture, in contrast to the abstract diagrams of functionalism! Figural architecture, hence, does not consist of casual inventions, but of *typical* elements which may be repeated, combined and varied. We have already suggested that the typical elements are not just a matter of con-

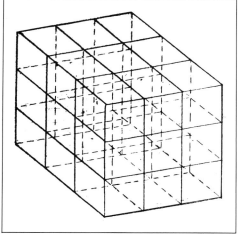

vention, but represent basic ways of being between earth and sky. They are given with the world, like spoken language, and the task of the architect consists in making them appear at the right moment and in the right place, that is, "as something." When that happens, the type becomes a concrete figure. The type, as such, does not exist, only its figural manifestations. But it has a name, whereas the individual figure has not. Hence it belongs to the general ground on which all phenomena appear. This does not mean that it is an abstraction, like "volume" or "proportion." It is eminently concrete. When we say "tower," "dome" and "column," we refer to a real entity which may be set into work.

The types which remain constant during history, may be called "archetypes," as they have general validity. The archetypes, however, disappear and appear again. The dome, for instance, did not play any important role in Western architecture during the Middle Ages, although it did not entirely disappear. What is important, is that archetypes become subject to ever new interpretations. A tower always stands up in space, but what does it mean to stand up *here and now*? Which is the towering figure which expresses *this* standing? Evidently interpretations do not change completely from case to case. Local and temporal circumstances have a certain stability, and hence we may talk about local and historical types, such as the "Emmental roof" or the "Gothic spire." This implies that particular *memories* are added to the archetypal figure.

The interpretation or the setting-into-work of a type consists in a process of articulation, that is, of defining constituent elements and subordinate parts. Through this process a basic way of being between earth and sky is elucidated

139. Dome: S. Maria delle Carceri, Prato.

and varied. The vertical soar of a tower may thus be emphasized or softened, or a conflict between resting and rising may be expressed. We have already pointed out that the artistic form is capable of comprising logical contradictions. Thus it may be simultaneously heavy and light, static and dynamic, or, in Robert Venturi's words, it may be "both-and."[164] Articulation, however, should not be carried to a point when the type is deprived of its identity. In that case figural quality would be lost. The type has in other words to be respected to be contradicted!

To understand the nature of typology, it is not enough to refer to the general ways of being between earth and sky. We also have to remember that they always take place "as something." We do not here refer to the local and temporal manifestations, but rather to the categories of collective, public and private dwelling. Thus we ought to investigate the archetypes of collective being in the world, of public being in the world and of private being in the world. Evidently these are varieties of the general archetypes or represent choices between them. The tower, thus, is primarily used as a public form, whereas the urban topological enclosure suits collectivity.

We realize that dwelling depends on typology. To gain an existential foothold in relation to things, to others and to himself, man needs an architecture which reveals his understanding of the world. This understanding comprises both an intuition of what is general and a knowledge of what is circumstantial. The general understanding is stored in the types, whereas the circumstantial knowledge is expressed by the concrete architectural figure which sets the type into work. Type and work correspond to language and discourse, and hence to the "house of Being" and its

manifestations. Man therefore does not only dwell in urban spaces and buildings, but also in the language of architecture. It is in fact this dwelling which makes all the others possible.

Language today

The loss of the built form and the spatial figure is not only a result of a weakened understanding of the nature of form and space, but first of all of the abolishment of the language of architecture. The slogan "form follows function" does not admit the existence of any typological ground, but asserts that the forms are constituted anew over and over again. At most it recognizes the existence of certain "traditions." The loss of language stems from the general trend towards abstraction which distinguishes our epoch. Thus we reduce reality to what is measurable, and transform concrete place into abstract space. As a result the daily life-world fades away, and man becomes a foreigner among things. The faculty of imagination is killed, that is, the ability to understand the world in terms of figures which are rooted in typology. Husserl pointed out this danger in his criticism of Western science, and as a remedy launched the slogan "to the things themselves!" Thus he advocated a return to what is concrete; an aim which has been followed up by Heidegger, Merleau-Ponty, Bachelard, Bollnow and others. Today, however, we experience the promise of a return to figurative architecture. The problems of typology and meaning are much discussed, and the need for a common language is recognized.[165] The question of memory has also come to the fore, since any meaningful form necessarily is something that "reminds." Thus the forms of the past are back again as possible choices, in particular the classical ones, because the classical

133

language represents the most universal and coherent figurative system so far known.[166] The danger is evidently a relapse into superficial historicism. Already Giedion, however, recognized the difference between using history as a "department store" of motifs and as a source of "constituent facts." But he did not understand the nature of the latter as interpretations of man's being between earth and sky. Even the present advocates of figurative "post-modernism" hardly grasp the existential nature of type and figure, and therefore easily become victims of a new eclecticism.[167] To face this danger, we have to come to terms with the meaning of Husserl's slogan. "To the things themselves" implies that we recover man's natural understanding of things as modes of being-in-the-world, that is, as gatherings. Accordingly we have to develop our poetical intuition and intend the world in terms of qualities rather than quantities. This does not mean that we reduce our understanding to spontaneous intuition. By means of the phenomenological method, we may "think" about things and disclose their "thingness." As an essay in phenomenology, the present book illustrates this approach. Phenomenology ought to become the gathering middle of education, and hence the means which may help us to recover the poetic awareness which is the essence of dwelling. What we need, in general, is a rediscovery of the world, in the sense of respect and care. We do not improve our situation through great "plans," but by taking care of what is close to us, that is, of things. "The things trust us for rescue," Rilke says.[168] But we can only rescue the things if we first have taken them into our hearts. When that happens, we *dwell*, in the true sense of the word.

Notes to the text

1. T. Vesaas, *Vindane*, Oslo 1952.

2. T. Vesaas, *Huset of fuglen*, Oslo 1971.

3. M. Heidegger, *Being and Time*, (1927), New York 1962, p. 83.

4. A. de Saint-Exupéry, *The Wisdom of the Sands*, London 1948.

5. E. Rubin, *Visuell wahrgenommene Figuren*, Copenhagen 1921.

6. K. Lynch, *The Image of the City*, Cambridge, Mass. 1960.

7. E. Husserl, *Die Krisis der europäischen Wissenschaften*, (1935), The Hague 1954.

8. M. Merleau-Ponty, *Phenomenology of Perception*, (1945), London 1962, p. 324.

9. Ibidem, p. 319.

10. Ibidem, p. 320.

11. Ibidem, p. 322.

12. M. Heidegger, "The Thing," in *Poetry, Language, Thought*, New York 1971, pp. 165 ff.

13. Ibidem, p. 179.

14. M. Heidegger, "The Origin of the Work of Art," in *Poetry...*, cit., pp. 17 ff.

15. M. Heidegger, "Poetically Man Dwells," in *Poetry...*, cit., p. 215.

16. Ibidem, p. 218.

17. M. Heidegger, "Building Dwelling Thinking," in *Poetry...*, cit., p. 149.

18. M. Heidegger, *Hebel der Hausfreund*, Pfullingen 1957, p. 13.

19. C. Norberg-Schulz, *Genius Loci*, Milan-New York 1979.

20. K. Lynch, op. cit., pp. 4, 5.

21. C. Norberg-Schulz, *Existence, Space and Architecture*, London 1971.

22. O.F. Bollnow, *Mensch und Raum*, Stuttgart 1963, p. 58.

23. M. Eliade, *The Sacred and the Profane*, New York 1959, pp. 20 ff.

24. Le Corbusier, *Towards a New Architecture*, London 1927, p. 173.

25. K. Lynch, op. cit.

26. W. Müller, *Die heilige Stadt*, Stuttgart 1961, p. 38.

27. C. Norberg-Schulz, "Khan, Heidegger and the Language of Architecture," in *Oppositions 18*, Cambridge, Mass. 1979.

28. M. Heidegger, "Building Dwelling Thinking," in *Poetry...*, cit., p. 154.

29. C. Norberg-Schulz, *Existence...*, cit., p. 21.

30. C. Norberg-Schulz, *Intentions in Architecture*, London-Oslo 1963, p. 44.

31. B. Jager, "Horizontality and Verticality," in *Duquesne Studies in Phenomenological Psychology*, vol. I, 1971.

32. J. Jacobi, *The Psychology of C.G. Jung*, New Haven 1951, p. 53.

33. M. Heidegger, "Language," in *Poetry...*, cit., pp. 189 ff.

34. M. Heidegger, "Poetically Man Dwells," in *Poetry...*, cit., p. 226. Also C. Norberg-Schulz, "Heidegger's Thinking on Architecture," in *Perspecta 20*, New Haven 1983, pp. 61 ff.

35. The word "settlement" is here used to designate dwelling places on different environmental levels: farm, village, town, city.

36. V. Scully, *The Earth, the Temple and the Gods*, New Haven 1962.

37. C. Norberg-Schulz, *Genius Loci*, cit.

38. See for instance *Merian Europa*, Kassel-Basel 1965.

39. See however S. von Moos, *Turm und Bollwerk*, Zürich 1974.

40. Tower houses were much used in various European countries during the Middle Ages. Well known are the slender towers of northern and central Italy, and the square tower-houses of Scotland.

41. C. Norberg-Schulz. *Existence...*, cit.

42. Id., *Intentions...*, cit., p. 43.

43. Id., *Existence...*, cit., p. 78.

44. Id., *Meaning in Western Architecture*, London 1974, ch. I.

45. D. Bahat, *Carta's Historical Atlas of Jerusalem*, Jerusalem 1983, p. 35.

46. C. Norberg-Schulz, *Genius Loci*, cit., p. 69.

47. The Italian word *veduta* means something seen.

48. C. Norberg-Schulz, *Genius Loci*, cit., p. 42.

49. Ibidem, pp. 180 ff.

50. Ibidem, pp. 138 ff.

51. Le Corbusier, *La Maison des Hommes*, Paris 1942.

52. C. Norberg-Schulz, *Roots of Modern Architecture*, Tokyo 1985.

53. V. Scully, *Louis I. Kahn*, New York 1962, p. 12.

54. L. Wittgenstein, *Tractatus locico-philosophicus*, 1921.

55. K. Lynch, op. cit., pp. 46 ff.

56. The German concepts were introduced by H. Sedlmayr.

57. In the past many cities were distinguished by particular pavement patterns.

58. K. Lynch, op. cit. See his various diagrammatic plans.

59. R. Krier, *Stadtraum*, Stuttgart 1975.

60. P. Zucker, *Town and Square*, New York 1959, p. 1.

61. The French word for the square in front of a church, *parvis*, stems from "paradise."

62. Like in the works of Sibelius.

63. A.E. Brinckmann, *Deutsche Stadtbaukunst*, Frankfurt 1911; id., *Platz und Monument*, Berlin 1912; R. Unwin, *Town Planning in Practice*, London 1909.

64. R. Krier, op. cit.

65. C. Sitte, *Der Städtebau*, Vienna 1909, p. 2.

66. See P. Zucker, op. cit., for a typology of squares.

67. K. Lynch, op. cit.

68. Also many "theoretical" plans from the nineteenth century.

69. We may also remind of the famous *vedute* by Bellotto.

70. A. Boethius, *The Golden House of Nero*, Ann Arbor 1960, pp. 129 ff.

71. R. Venturi, *Complexity and Contradiction in Architecture*, New York 1966, p. 88.

72. P. Zucker, op. cit.

73. A.E. Brinckmann, *Platz...*, cit., p. 18.

74. S. Bianca, *Architektur und Lebensform im islamischen Stadtwesen*, Zürich 1975.

75. L. Hilberseimer, *The New City*, Chicago 1944.

76. K. Lynch, op. cit., p. 41.

77. A. Rossi, *L'architettura della città*, Padua 1966.

78. C. Terrasse, *La cathédrale miroir du monde*, Paris 1946.

79. R. Venturi, op. cit.

80. C. Norberg-Schulz, *Michelangelo som arkitekt*, Oslo 1958.

81. The concept of "leading building task" was introduced by H. Sedlmayr in *Verlust der Mitte*, Salzburg 1948.

82. Ibidem.

83. V. Scully, *The Earth...*, cit., passim.

84. In German the word *bauen* means to cultivate the land as well as to erect buildings. The farmer is a *Bauer*, that is, "builder."

85. C. Norberg-Schulz, *Genius Loci*, cit.

86. Id., "Le ultime intenzioni di Alberti," in *Acta Institutum Romanum Norvegiae*, vol. I, Rome 1962.

87. C. Norberg-Schulz, *Meaning...*, cit., ch. 6.

88. E. Dyggve, *Dödekult, keiserkult og basilika*, Oslo 1943.

89. C. Norberg-Schulz, *Baroque Architecture*, New York 1971, p. 217.

90. Id., *K.I. Dientzenhofer e il barocco boemo*, Rome 1968.

91. Id., *Baroque...*, cit.

92. Id., *Roots...*, cit.

93. Hans Scharoun, *Akademie der Künste*, Berlin 1967.

94. R. Schwarz, *Vom Bau der Kirche*, Heidelberg 1947, p. 46.

95. E. Guidoni, *La città europea*, Milan 1980.

96. Le Corbusier *Towards...*, cit., p. 31.

97. Ibidem, p. 147.

98. Such as the wish of Louis XIV to add a dome to his palace in Versailles.

99. We may also remind of the open-air chapel of Hildebrandt at Göllersdorf.(1725).

100. C. Norberg-Schulz, *Roots...*, cit.

101. S. Giedion, *Architecture, You and Me*, Cambridge, Mass. 1958, p. 28.

102. C. Norberg-Schulz, *Kahn...*, cit.

103. Id., *Roots...*, cit., ch. 5.

104. G. Bachelard, *Poetics of Space*, (1958), Boston 1964.

105. M. Heidegger, *Being...*, cit., p. 176.

106. O.F. Bollnow, *Vom Vesen der Stimmungen*, Frankfurt a.M. 1956, p. 33.

107. M. Heidegger, *Being...*, cit., p. 182.

108. C. Norberg-Schulz, *Kahn...*, cit.

109. F.L. Wright, *The Natural House*, (1954), New York 1970, p. 32.

110. L. Binswanger, *Grundformen und Erkenntnis menschlichen Daseins*, Munich 1962, p. 25.

111. The German word *Erinnerung* means something which has been "taken in," "internalized."

112. C. Norberg-Schulz, Y. Futagawa, M. Suzuki, *Wooden Houses in Europe*, Tokyo 1978.

113. L.B. Alberti, *De re aedificatoria*, IX, ii.

114. C. Norberg-Schulz, *Genius Loci*, cit.

115. Ibidem, pp. 66 ff.

116. It was, however, prepared for by suburban villas of the Renaissance and Baroque.

117. C. Norberg-Schulz, *Casa Behrens*, Rome 1980.

118. F.L. Wright, op. cit., p. 16.

119. L. Veltheim-Lottum, *Kleine Weltgeschichte des städtischen Wohnhauses*, Heidelberg 1952.

120. Le Corbusier, *Towards...*, cit., pp. 169 ff.

121. M.H. Baillie-Scott, *Houses and Gardens*, London 1906, p. 18.

122. Ibidem, p. 2.

123. Ibidem, p. 54.

124. Such as Robert A.M. Stern.

125. C. Moore, G. Allen, D. Lyndon, *The Place of Houses*, New York 1974, p. 82.

126. C. Norberg-Schulz, *Roots...*, cit.

127. L. Moholy-Nagy, *The New Vision*, New York 1946, p. 59.

128. V. Scully, *The Shingle Style*, New Haven 1971, pp. 162 ff.

129. A. Boethius, op. cit.

130. J. Trier, First. *Gesellschaft der Wissenschaften zu Göttingen*, 1940, p. 117.

131. S. Giedion, *Befreites Wohnen*, Zürich 1929, p. 9.

132. Le Corbusier, *La Maison...*, cit.

133. F.R.S. Yorke, *The Modern House*, London 1934; id., *The Modern Flat*, London 1937.

134. *Global Architecture 39*, Tokyo 1976.

135. C. Moore, G. Allen, D. Lyndon, op. cit.

136. M. Heidegger, "Letter on Humanism," in *Basic Writings*, New York 1977; id. "Language," in *Poetry...*, cit., pp. 189 ff.

137. M. Heidegger, *Being...*, cit., p. 203.

138. M. Heidegger, "Language," in *Poetry...*, cit., pp. 190, 210.

139. G. Broadbent, R. Bunt, C. Jencks, *Signs, Symbols and Architecture*, Chichester 1980.

140. M. Heidegger, "Poetically Man Dwells," in *Poetry...*, cit., pp. 221 ff.

141. Ibidem, p. 218.

142. M. Heidegger, "The Thing," in *Poetry...*, cit., p. 179.

143. M. Heidegger, "Poetically Man Dwells," in *Poetry...*, cit., p. 225.

144. Ibidem, p. 208.

145. M. Heidegger, *Being...*, cit., pp. 149 ff.

146. As is maintained by semiological theory. See Broadbent et al., op. cit.

147. Baillie-Scott, op. cit., p. 40.

148. M. Heidegger, "The Origin of the Work of Art," in *Poetry...*, cit., p. 64.

149. Ibidem, p. 63.

150. Ibidem, p. 63.

151. Ibidem, pp. 41 ff.

152. We may remind of Vasari's description of Brunelleschi's dome.

153. M.G. van Rensselaer, *Henry Hobson Richardson and His Works*, New York 1888.

154. C. Norberg-Schulz, *Intentions...*, cit., p. 164.

155. Ibidem, chapter on "Technics."

156. Id., *Genius Loci...*, cit., chapter on Prague.

157. M. Heidegger, *Hebel...*, cit., p. 7.

158. V. Scully, *The Earth...*, cit.; also C. Norberg-Schulz, *Meaning...*, cit., ch. 2.

159. R. Arnheim, *Art and Visual Perception*, Berkeley-Los Angeles 1954.

160. The concepts of "addition" and "division" were introduced by P. Frankl, *Entwicklungsphasen der neueren Baukunst*, Leipzig-Berlin 1914.

161. C. Norberg-Schulz, *Intentions...*, cit.

162. Id., *Architetture di Paolo Portoghesi e Vittorio Gigliotti*, Rome 1982.

163. G.C. Manson, *Frank Lloyd Wright to 1910*, New York 1958, pp. 6 ff.

164. R. Venturi, op. cit.

165. C. Norberg-Schulz, *Roots...*, cit., ch. 8

166. C. Jencks, "Post-Modern Classicism," in *Architectural Design*, 5/6, 1980.

167. Such as J. Stirling in his museum in Stuttgart.

168. R.M. Rilke, *Duinese Elegies* IX.

Index of names and places